ARAMAIC TEXTS FROM QUMRAN

SEMITIC STUDY SERIES

NEW SERIES EDITED BY

J. H. HOSPERS, T. JANSMA AND G. F. PIJPER

Nº IV

ARAMAIC TEXTS FROM QUMRAN

WITH TRANSLATIONS AND ANNOTATIONS

BY

B. JONGELING
C. J. LABUSCHAGNE
A. S. VAN DER WOUDE

VOLUME I

TUTA SUB AEGIDE PALLAS · EJB ·

LEIDEN
E. J. BRILL
1976

ISBN 90 04 04452 3

PRINTED IN THE NETHERLANDS

TABLE OF CONTENTS

PREFACE

The present volume aims at providing students with a relatively cheap, and handy tool for the study of some of the most interesting Aramaic documents from Qumran. Furthermore, it might prove to be useful to scholars who are not specialists in the field of Dead Sea Scrolls study. By consequence this publication is meant to be a counterpart to Eduard Lohse's well-known book *Die Texte aus Qumran. Hebräisch und Deutsch,* München and Darmstadt 1964. Though we find no justification for pointing the texts, as Lohse has done, we have decided to increase the notes for the benefit of students. Because the present publication cannot replace the standard editions of the texts, we do not indicate which letters are partly preserved in the manuscripts or whether they can be identified with certainty or not. On the other hand we have tried to improve on the transcriptions in the earlier editions at those points where we disagree with them. In some instances we have left gaps where questionable proposals are made in these editions.

We intend to publish an additional volume as soon as other major Aramaic documents from Qumran are made accessible to the scholarly world.

Groningen,
autumn 1975

B. Jongeling
C. J. Labuschagne
A. S. van der Woude

LIST OF ABBREVIATIONS

Aḥiqar	The Story of Aḥiqar (A. Cowley, *Aramaic Papyri of the Fifth Century*, Oxford, 1923, pp. 204-248).
AJA	*American Journal of Archaeology*, Cambridge Mass.
ANET	J. B. Pritchard, *Ancient Near Eastern Texts Relating to the Old Testament*, Princeton N.J., 1955².
ANET Suppl	J. B. Pritchard, *The Ancient Near East. Supplementary Texts and Pictures Relating to the Old Testament*, Princeton N.J., 1969.
Josephus BJ	Flavius Josephus, *Bellum Judaicum*.
BASOR	*Bulletin of the American Schools of Oriental Research*, New Haven Conn.
Bibl	*Biblica*, Rome.
B-L	H. Bauer und P. Leander, *Grammatik des Biblisch-Aramäischen*, Tübingen, 1927.
Brockelmann	C. Brockelmann, *Lexicon Syriacum*. Editio secunda et emendata, Halle, 1928.
Cowley	A. Cowley, *Aramaic Papyri of the Fifth Century*, Oxford, 1923.
Dalman	G. Dalman, *Grammatik des jüdisch-palästinischen Aramäisch*, Leipzig, 1905².
DJD	*Discoveries in the Judaean Desert* (of Jordan), Oxford, 1955 ff.
Driver	G. R. Driver, *Aramaic Documents of the Fifth Century B.C.*, Oxford, 1954 (editio princeps); *Aramaic Documents of the Fifth Century B.C.* Abridged and revised edition, Oxford, 1957.
Fitzmyer	J. A. Fitzmyer, S. J., *The Genesis Apocryphon of Qumran Cave 1. A Commentary*, Rome, 1966, 1971².
HUCA	*Hebrew Union College Annual*, Cincinnati, Ohio.
Jastrow	M. Jastrow, *Dictionary of Talmud Babli, Yerushalmi, Midrashic Literature and Targumim*, I-II, New York, 1950.

JBL	*Journal of Biblical Literature*, Philadelphia Pa.
JNES	*Journal of Near Eastern Studies*, Chicago Ill.
JSS	*Journal of Semitic Studies*, Manchester.
KUTSCHER	E. Y. KUTSCHER, *The Language of the "Genesis Apocryphon". A preliminary study*, Scripta Hierosolymitana IV (edd. CH. RABIN and Y. YADIN), Jerusalem, 1958, 1965².
LEANDER *ÄgAr*	P. LEANDER, *Laut- und Formenlehre des Ägyptisch-Aramäischen*, Göteborg, 1928; reprint Hildesheim, 1966.
LXX	Septuagint.
MT	Masoretic Text.
Pesh	Peshiṭta.
1QGenAp	The Genesis Apocryphon of Qumran Cave 1.
1QpHab	The Habakkuk Commentary of Qumran Cave 1.
4QOrNab	The Prayer of Nabonidus of Qumran Cave 4.
11QtgJob	The Job Targum of Qumran Cave 11.
RB	*Revue Biblique*, Paris.
RQum	*Revue de Qumrân*, Paris.
ScrHier	Scripta Hierosolymitana.
Sefire	The Aramaic Inscriptions of Sefire (J. A. FITZMYER, S. J., *The Aramaic Inscriptions of Sefîre*, Rome, 1967).
tg 2	The Job Targum, edited by P. DE LAGARDE, *Hagiographa Chaldaice*, Lipsiae, 1873; reprint Osnabrück, 1967.
TJ	Targum Jonathan.
TO	Targum Onkelos.
VT	*Vetus Testamentum*, Leiden.
ZAW	*Zeitschrift für die Alttestamentliche Wissenschaft*, Berlin.
ZDMG	*Zeitschrift der Deutschen Morgenländischen Gesellschaft*, Wiesbaden.

THE JOB TARGUM FROM CAVE 11

(11QtgJob)

INTRODUCTION

In 1961 the Dutch *Royal Academy of Sciences* procured the rights from the *Palestine Archaeological Museum* in Jerusalem to study and publish a number of manuscripts from cave 11 of Qumran. This cave, discovered by Bedouin in 1956, contained a very large number of manuscripts which became the property of the museum. The largest and most important manuscript obtained by the Royal Academy is an Aramaic translation of several passages in the book of Job.

Unfortunately, because of damage to the manuscript, only about 15% of the text of the book of Job in Aramaic, which must have been complete in former times, has survived. The end of the manuscript, containing fragmentary passages of Job xxxvii, 10 — xlii, 11, is still in the form of a scroll. This so-called "small scroll" is 109 cm long, 4 to 6 cm high and has 10 columns of which the upper line is lacking wholly or partly and some of the lower lines are completely or partly lost. Of the preceding section of the manuscript only 27 smaller or larger fragments have survived,[1] containing passages from Job xvii, 14—xxxvi, 33. Besides these there are some very small fragments of not more than a few letters each, most of which can be inserted in the text.

---

[1] It is interesting to note that 'fragment 1' consists of two fragments put together.

The extant Aramaic text is a fairly faithful rendering of the Hebrew book of Job. It does not have the elaborations typical of the other Targums.[2] In a few instances it offers a longer text, but in several instances a shorter one.[3] On the whole we may assume that this Aramaic book of Job was as long as the original Hebrew book. Seeing that the scroll contained 34 columns[4] from the middle of the book (chapter xxii between the verses 15 and 16) onwards, the entire scroll must have contained about 68 columns. Each column had some 16 or 17 lines.

The script is of the type labelled by ALBRIGHT as "Herodian" (37 B.C.E.—70 C.E.).[5] CROSS dated two manuscripts palaeographically resembling the Job Targum to about 50 C.E.[6] The evidence points to

---

[2] This is the usual term denoting the Aramaic translations of the books of the Old Testament.

[3] Longer: Column XIV, 1 (Job xxix 7); XIX, 4-6 (xxxi 29); XXIII, 2 (xxxiii 25); XXXVII, 5.6 (after xlii 2). Shorter: II, 2-3 (xix 13.14); V, 4-5 (xxi 23-24); XVIII, 3 (xxxi 10); XXII, 6 (xxxiii 12); XXV, 2 (xxxiv 25-26); XXXIII, 5 (xxxix 24); XXXVII, 5-6 (after xlii 2).

[4] Of these 34 columns 32 have survived, however, incomplete. A comparison between the Hebrew and the Aramaic text shows that there must have been two columns between the present columns VII and VIII, and that there must have been a column between I and II, and between III and IV.

[5] W. F. ALBRIGHT, A Biblical Fragment from the Maccabaean Age: The Nash Papyrus, *JBL* 56 (1937), 145-176.

[6] F. M. CROSS, The Development of the Jewish Scripts, *The Bible and the Ancient Near East*, Essays in Honor of

the first century C.E., towards the end of the "Herodian" period, for the origin of the manuscript. The script is clear and can be read easily. Except for the instances where they are used in ligatures, the letters *waw* and *yod* are not similar. This goes for *beth* and *kaf* and for *daleth* and *reš* too.

Even more important than the problem of the date of the manuscript is the question of the date of the extant text. Here the language is a decisive factor. Research into the language of the Job Targum has shown that the language of this Targum is older than that of the Genesis Apocryphon from cave 1, but younger than that of the book of Daniel.[7] According to KUTSCHER the former must be dated to the first century B.C.E.,[8] and since the latter dates

---

William Foxwell Albright, New York 1961, 133-202. See also N. AVIGAD, The Palaeography of the Dead Sea Scrolls and Related Documents, *Aspects of the Dead Sea Scrolls* (ScrHier 4), Jerusalem 1958, 1965², 56-87.

[7] The *nota relationis* in 11QtgJob is always *dy*, like in Daniel and Ezra; in 1QGenAp the younger form *d-* occurs next to the more common *dy*. The causative is formed in 11QtgJob, like in Biblical Aramaic, by means of *h* in most cases, but also by means of ʾ, like in 1QGenAp. The same pattern is followed with regard to the reflexive forms *ht/ʾt*. The Job Targum and Biblical Aramaic use the conjunction *hn* 'if, when', whereas 1QGenAp uses *ʾn*. 1QGenAp knows *kmn* besides *kmʾ* (*kmh*) 'how'; 11QtgJob has always *kmʾ*. Likewise 1QGenAp has *tmn* instead of *tmh* 'there', but 11QtgJob and Biblical Aramaic have *tmh*. On the other hand our Targum has the demonstrative *dn*, which is a younger form than *dnʾ*, but 1QGenAp and other Aramaic Qumran texts use as a rule *dn* and Biblical Aramaic *dnh*.

[8] E. Y. KUTSCHER, The Language of the "Genesis Apo-

from the first half of the second century B.C.E., that of the Job Targum can be dated to the second half of the second century B.C.E.

This means that the Aramaic book of Job is the oldest known Targum. Evidence from Jewish literature shows that written Targums existed in fairly early times, after the period in which there was an oral targum tradition.[9] Most important in this respect is the reference to an Aramaic book of Job in both the Jerusalem and the Babylonian Talmud,[10] where it is told that this book was taken out of circulation by Rabbi Gamaliel the elder, who flour-

---

cryphon", *Aspects of the Dead Sea Scrolls* (ScrHier 4), Jerusalem 1958, 1965², 1-35.

[9] For a general introduction to the Targum literature see R. LE DÉAUT, *Introduction à la littérature targumique* I, Rome 1966, who discusses written Targums on pp. 52 ff.

[10] Shabbath XVI, 1 (bShabbath 115a; jShabbath 15c); see also TosShabbath XIII (M. S. ZUCKERMANDEL, *Tosephta*, New Edition, Jerusalem 1970, p. 128), Sopherîm V and XVI. The Palestinian Talmud reads: "R. Gamaliel was standing on a terrace of the temple mound and they brought him a targum of the book of Job. He summoned a mason who hid it under a layer of stones".

The Babylonian Talmud offers a more detailed account: "R. Jose said: My father once visited R. Ḥalaphta at Rabban Gamaliel Berabbi in Tiberias; he found him sitting at a table with Johanan the excommunicated and reading a Job targum he had in his hand. He said to him: I remember that your grandfather Rabban Gamaliel, when he stood on a terrace of the temple mound and they brought him a targum of the book of Job, said to a mason: Put it under a layer of stones. On this order he hid it. Then he (Gamaliel II) also let it be hidden." The text in the Tosephta differs from that of the Babylonian Talmud on a few minor points.

ished between 25 and 50 C.E. During his days a written Targum of the book of Job already existed, a fact corroborated by the Qumran discovery. The Targum, referred to in the Talmud, could have been a copy of the newly found one. No reason is given for the withdrawal of the book from circulation, but it might have been because of its heterodox provenance.

The Hebrew text, of which 11QtgJob is the Aramaic translation, resembles the Masoretic text very closely. Differences can mostly be explained as due to the targumist's translation technique, or to his theological considerations, or to a misreading by the translator (or the copyist), or to a wrong interpretation of a word. On the other hand there are differences, which cannot be explained in this way, and which lead one to conclude that the targumist's Hebrew original differed from the Masoretic text. In some instances where 11QtgJob differs from the Masoretic text it corresponds with the Septuagint, the ancient Greek translation of the Old Testament. The following examples show differences owing to theological (or ethical) considerations:

1. In column X, 2 we read: 'The pillars of heaven He causes to tremble', which is the rendering of Job xxvi 11a 'The pillars of heaven tremble'. The targumist seems to stress God's might and sovereign power.

2. The idea of creation is a recurrent feature, e.g. in XXIV, 7 (Job xxxiv 13: 'It is He who made the

earth', where MT has 'Who entrusted the earth to Him?'.

3. In XVIII, 3 the targumist left out the second half of Job xxxi 10, probably because he found the passage shocking. The MT reads: (9) If my heart has been enticed by a woman, or if I have hidden myself at my neighbour's door, (10) let my wife grind for another, and others bend over her'.

4. XXX, 4-5 reads: '...when shone together the morning-stars and exulted together all the angels of God', whereas the MT (Job xxxviii 7)has: 'While the morning-stars sang together and all the sons of God exulted'. It is clear that here the targumist deliberately rationalizes the figurative language of the original text.

5. In XXXIV, 4 God asks Job: 'Would you set aside the judgment...?', but the Hebrew text reads: 'Would you annul my judgment...?'. The targumist wants to preclude the idea of man being able to annul God's judgment.

6. The most significant difference between the Hebrew book of Job and the present Job Targum is the way in which the figure of Job is pictured towards the end of the book. In the Bible Job is depicted as remorseful, because he failed to recognize God's sovereign power, in spite of the fact that his case was just. The MT reads: 'So I recant and repent in dust and ashes' (Job xlii 6), but the Targum has: 'Therefore I am poured out and I fall to pieces, and I am dust and ashes' (XXXVII, 8). Thus in the targumist's

picture of him Job continues to be the innocent sufferer.[11]

The Septuagint contains an addition at the end of the book of Job, beginning with the words: 'This one ἑρμηνεύεται from the Syrian (or Aramaic) book...', in which something is said about Job's pedigree and genealogy. The term ἑρμηνεύεται, which also occurs in Hebr. vii 2, means something like 'These are the personalia of...'. The Septuagint translators got these personal details about Job from a Syrian (or Aramaic) source. This source must have been another than the Qumran Targum, which does not have such an addition at the end. The scroll contains the text up to chapter xlii 11, but the rest of the column could have contained the rest of the chapter (MT verses 12-17). Next to this column there is a section of the scroll on which nothing is written, a blank 'page' at the end of the scroll. It is even possible, though not certain, that the Targum ended at verse 11, where a paragraph ends. But this may also be the end of a larger pericope, which the translator ends in the same way, as in the case of the discourses by Job, by his friends or by God. Judged by the contents, chapter xlii 12 could just as well have been the beginning of a new passage.

---

[11] For a detailed study of the Hebrew, Aramaic and Greek text, see E. W. Tuinstra, *Hermeneutische aspecten van de targum van Job uit grot XI van Qumrân*, diss. Groningen, 1970.

The discovery of the Job Targum and of other Aramaic texts is a matter of great importance in more than one respect. First, it fills the gap in our knowledge of Aramaic, a gap of several centuries, probably five hundred years, between the Aramaic of the books of Daniel and Ezra and that of the Palestinian Aramaic dialects known to us. In all probability the Aramaic spoken by Jesus came very close to the Aramaic of Qumran.

Second, the discovery sheds light on the Targums and their history, a field of study on which Old and New Testament scholars focus more and more attention. The Job Targum proves beyond doubt that written Targums existed at a relatively early time, at about 100 B.C.E., and is itself a specimen of this type of literature at a fairly early stage of its development, showing how people of those days read and interpreted a Biblical book.

Third, the Targum is an important factor to scholars who study the text of the Bible. It is a new piece of material and a new aid to textual criticism, offering some variant readings and shedding light on the prehistory of the Masoretic text.

LITERATURE

Editio princeps:

Le Targum de Job de la grotte XI de Qumrân, édité et traduit par J. P. M. van der Ploeg, O.P. et A. S. van der Woude, avec la collaboration de B. Jongeling, Leiden 1971.

Preliminary Communications:

J. van der Ploeg, Le Targum de Job de la grotte 11 de Qumran, *Mededelingen der Koninklijke Nederlandse Akademie van Wetenschappen*, afd. Letterkunde, Nieuwe Reeks, deel 25, no. 9, Amsterdam 1962, pp. 545-557.

A. S. van der Woude, Das Hiobtargum aus Höhle XI, *Congress Volume Bonn 1962* (Supplements to VT IX), Leiden 1963, pp. 322-331. English translation in *The Australian Journal of Biblical Archaeology* 1, no. 2 (1969), pp. 19-29.

Further Literature:

A. Dupont-Sommer, Notes qoumrâniennes: 1) sur 11QtgJob, col. XXXIII (this should be XXXVIII), *Semitica* 15 (1965), pp. 71-74.

J. A. Fitzmyer, Some Observations on the Targum of Job from Qumran Cave 11, *The Catholic Biblical Quarterly* 36 (1974), pp. 503-524.

G. Fohrer, 4QOrNab, 11QtgJob und die Hioblegende, *ZAW* 75 (1963), pp. 93-97.

B. Jongeling, Contributions of the Qumran Job Targum to the Aramaic Vocabulary, *JSS* 17 (1972), pp. 191-197.

B. Jongeling, The Job Targum from Qumran Cave 11 (11QtgJob), *Folia Orientalia* 15 (1974), pp. 181-196.

B. Jongeling, *Een Aramees boek Job uit de bibliotheek van Qumrân* (Exegetica, nieuwe reeks, no. 3), Amsterdam 1974.

S. Segert, Sprachliche Bemerkungen zu einigen aramäischen Texten von Qumrân, *Archiv Orientální* 33 (1965), pp. 190-206.

M. Sokoloff, *The Targum to Job from Qumran Cave XI*, Bar-Ilan University, Ramat-Gan, 1974.

E. W. Tuinstra, *Hermeneutische aspecten van de Targum van Job uit grot XI van Qumrân*, diss. Groningen, 1970.

R. Weiss, Further Notes on the Qumran Targum to Job, *JSS* 19 (1974), pp. 13-18.

COLUMN I

(fragm. 1a + 1b; Job xvii 14-xviii 4)

1 (14)לתולע]תה [15]ומא אפו א[סבר וסברתי מן
2 יחזנה][16]העמי לשאול ת[נחת או כחדא
3 בעפר נ]שכב
4 xviii [1] ענ]א בלדד שוחא[ה ואמר [2]עד
5 אימת]י תשוא סוף למלא[
6 [3]למה לב]עירא דמינא[[4]
7] העל דב[רתך
8]מקאת[רה [5]

COLUMN II

(fragm. 2; Job xix 11-19)

1 [11]ותק]ף עלי רגזה וח[שבני [12]
2 י]תון חתפוהי וכבשו[[13/14]
3 הרחקו וידעי ב·[[15]
4 ביתי אמתי לנכר[

I

1 *'pw*: an emphasizing particle, often used in Biblical Hebrew; cf. IV, 3; IX, 2; Aḥiqar, 52.140.

2 *tnḥt:* if this conjecture is correct, the verbal form may be a 3rd pers. fem. imperf., the subject being *sbrty* « my hope ».

3 *nškb*: if this is the correct reading, the subject « we » may include "I" and "my hope".

4 *šwḥ'h*: gentilicium, cf. DALMAN, p. 177; B-L, § 13k.

5 *'d 'ymty*: conjecture based on TJ Hab. i 2.

7 *'l dbrtk*: cf. XXXIV, 4 and Dan. ii 30; iv 14.

Column I
Job xvii 14-xviii 4

[14] *I have said to corruption*: *'you are my father'*;
'you are my mother and my sister', 1 *to* the *maggot*.
[15] And what ever do I *hope?* 2 *And my hope, who*
shall see it? [16] Will it *go down* with me to Sheol? *or* 3
shall *we* lie down *together in the dust?*
4 [xviii] [1] Bildad the Shuhit*e began to s*p*e*ak *and said*: 5
[2] *Wh*e*n* will you stop speaking? *Be wise and then*
we may talk. 6 [3] *Why* are we lik*e ca*ttle .....[4].... 7
.... Is it for *your* sa*k*e 8
.... out of *its* pla*ce*? [5].................

Column II
Job xix 11-19

1 [11]*And* his anger *fla*red up against me and He
c*ounted me one of his enemies*. [12]*Together* 2 *c*ome his
raiders and level *their path against me*. [13/14]*My brethren*
from me 3 they have removed, and my acquaintances
.... [15]*The guests of* 4 my house, (even)

II

1 *tqp rgz*: usual targumic rendering of Hebr. *ḥārāh 'ap*, cf. Jastrow, *s.v. tqp*.
2 *ytwn*: 3rd pers. plur. imperf. of *'t'*.
3 *wyd'y*: in view of the limited space available in this line and of the contents of line 4 it is most probable to suppose that the targumist's eye skipped from Hebr. *weyōde'ay* (vs. 13) to *ûmeyudā'ay* (vs. 14).
b.[: the reading *k*.[is not entirely excluded.
4 *'mty*: sing.; MT reads plur. (cf. LXX; Pesh).

5 [16]לעבדי קרית ולא ע[נא

6 [17]רוח המכת לאנתתי[[18]

7 רשיעין יסגפ[ונני [19]

8 כל אנש די[

Column III
(fragm. 3; Job xix 29-xx 6)

1 [(29)]]באיש

2 [

3 [xx 1]ענא צופר נעמאה והתי]ב [2]לכן לבבי י[תיבנני

4 [3] ק]ללתי אשמע ורו[ח

5 [4] יד]עת מן עלמא מן ד[י

6 בני אנשא על ארע]ה [5]ארו מבע רשיע[ין

7]לעבע תעדא [6][

8 ורשא]ה לענניא[[7]

6 *hmkt*: 1st pers. sing. perf. haphel of *mkk* « to lower ». The targumist altered the purport of MT.

8 It is not clear whether *dy* indicates a genitive construction by circumlocution or introduces a relative clause (with *dy* as subject or object).

III

1 Since the last part of line 1 and the whole of line 2 are left blank, *b'yš* is clearly the last word of the passage. Together with the lost words of line 1 it renders the latter part of the

my maid, *count me* a stranger, *I have become an alien in their eyes.* 5 [16]When I call my servant he gives no a*nswer* .... 6 [17]I have humiliated my spirit before my wife .... [18]*Even* 7 the wicked affl*ict me* .... [19]*They detest me,* 8 all people of (or: who(m ?)) ....

Column III
Job xix 29-xx 6

1 (29) .... bad. 2

3 xx [1]*Zophar the Naamathite began to speak and rep*lied: [2]Surely, my heart *cause*s *me to reply* 4 .... [3]*a rebuke that* curses me I hear, and a spir*it beyond* 5 *my comprehension answers me.* [4]*Do* you *kn*ow *this* from of old, sinc*e* 6 *man was placed on* the *earth*? [5]Behold, the rejoicing of the wick*ed* 7 *is brief and the gladness of the impious* passes away quickly. [6]*Though* 8 *his pride mounts up to heaven and* his *head reaches* unto the clouds
7 ....

enigmatic Hebrew text of Job xix 29 in a way which cannot be ascertained any more.

6 *ʾrw* in most cases corresponds to MT *kî*. The particle is attested in Dan. vii 2.5-7.13, and very often in this targum.
mbʿ: infinitive of *bwʿ*.

7 *lʿbʿ* « in a hurry »; cf. 1QGenAp XX, 9 (*lʿwbʿ*), and *lʿbq* in Egyptian Aramaic (Cowley 26, 6.22; 42, 7(bis). 8.13(bis); Driver ix, 3). See P. Grelot, *JSS* 1 (1956), pp. 202-205; *JSS* 2 (1957), p. 195. For *q* > ʿ cf. B-L, § 6c.

Column IV
(fragm. 4; Job xxi 2-10)

1 (2)למ[א לי להות .] 3
2 מנדעי תמיקון[4
3 ארו אפו לא ת[קצר רוחי 5
4 סימו ידיכון על [פומא 6
5 ותמהא אחד לי 7.]
6 והסגיו נכסין 8זרע[הון
7 לעיניהון 9בתיהון[
8 אלהא עליהו[ן 10
9 הריתהון פל[טת

Column V
(fragm. 5; Job xxi 20-27)

1 20 ע]ינוהי במפלתה ומ.[

IV

1 The meaning of *lhwt* is not clear. MT reads: « and let this be your consolations » (i.e. the consolations you give to me). In view of MT *zōʾt* the extant ʾ might be the final letter of the *pronomen demonstrativum dʾ*. LXX, however, renders: « lest there be for me the same consolation from you ». Both LXX and targum read « for me ». Supposing that the targum also contained « lest », one could fill up the lacuna by reading (*dy*) *lmʾ*. *lhwt* could be connected with *lhʾ* « to be tired, annoyed »; cf. also the substantive *lyʾw* (Jastrow, *s.v.*), and Syr. *lʾwtʾ*.

2 *mndʿy*: an instance of dissimilation (B-L, § 13d).

3 *ʾrw*: cf. III, 6. *ʾpw:* cf. I, 1. MT reads *weʾim maddûaʿ*,

Column IV
Job xxi 2-10

1 [2]*le*st (there be) annoyance (?) for me .... [3]*Bear*
with me while I speak, and after I have uttered 2 my
knowledge you may mock [4]......................
3 Behold, *my spirit* is not *impatient*, [5]...........
..... 4 lay your hands over *your mouth*. [6]*When I*
think of it, I become afraid, 5 and consternation
takes hold of me. [7]*How does it happen that the wicked*
live, grow old, 6 and increase their goods? [8]*Their*
posterity *is established before them, in their lifetime,*
and their offspring 7 before their eyes. [9]Their homes
are in safety, without fear, and not is the rod of 8
God upon the*m*. [10]*Their bull mounts and fails not*, 9
their pregnant (cow) cal*ves and does not miscarry*.

Column V
Job xxi 20-27

1 [20]*Let* his own *e*yes *see* his fall, and *let him drink* o*f*

which introduces the second part of a twofold question.

4 *ydykwn*: Ezra and the Elephantine papyri have the older suffix *-km* (cf. *-hm* for the 3rd pers. masc. plur.), but Daniel has already *-kwn* (and *-hwn*, cf. below, lines 7.9), due to contamination with the fem., and with lengthening of the vowel (cf. B-L, § 20v').

5 Perhaps *hyk* (cf. VII, 6) is to be read after *ly*.

9 *hrythwn*: fem. participle of *hr'* « to be pregnant », with the suffix 3rd pers. masc. plur. Cf. 1QGenAp II, 1.15; Sefire I A, 21. MT: « his cow »; LXX: ἐν γαστρὶ ἔχουσα.

V

1 *bmplth*: this is in accordance with the proposed reading in MT *pîdô*, instead of *kîdô*.

2 [21]]צבו לאלהא בביתה .[
3 מ]נין ירחוהי גזירין [22] הלא[להא
4 ו]הוא רמיא מדין (?) [24] אב.[
5 מו]ח גרמוהי [25] דן ימות בנפ[ש
6 ל]א אכל [26] כחדה על [
7 ע]ליהון [27] ארו ידעת[
8].י התעיטתון[[28]

Column VI

(fragm. 6 right side; Job xxii 3-9)

1 (2) [3] לא]להא
2]ארחך
3 [4] י]עול עמך
4 [5] ל]א איתי
5 [6] א]חיך מגן
6 [7]]צהא לא
7 ל]חם [8] ואמרת
8]אפוהי
9 [9] רי]קנה

4 *mdyn*: participle pael of *dyn*.

4/5 The targum is much shorter here than MT. The latter reads twice *zèh yāmût*, which may have caused confusion.

8 *htʿyṭtwn*: 2nd pers. plur. perf. hithpaal of *ʿwṭ* = *ʿwṣ*; cf. *ʿṭ* « counsel, advice ».

the wrath of the Almighty. 2 [21]*For what* interest has God in his house *after him,* 3 *when the nu*mber of his months is cut off? [22]Can *anyone teach* God 4 *knowledge,*(*God*) who judges the exalted ones? [24(?)] .... 5 .... *the mar*row of his bones. [25]He dies with a *bitter* soul, 6 *ne*ver having tasted *happiness.* [26]Together in *the dust they lie and the worms cover* 7 *t*hem. [27]Behold, I know *your thoughts* 8 *and the devices* you have plotted *against* me [28].................

Column VI
Job xxii 3-9

1 (2).................... [3]*Does it yield profit to* God 2 *that you are righteous, or is it gain to Him that you make* your conduct *perfect*? 3 [4]*Will He reprove you for your piety,* enter *into judgment* with you? 4 [5]*No, your wickedness is great and* there is *no* 5 *limit to your iniquities.* [6]*For you took a pledge from* your *br*others without reason, 6 *and stripped the clothing of the naked.* [7]*You gave the* thirsty no 7 *water and withheld b*read *from the hungry,* [8]and you said: 8 '*The earth belongs to the mighty man, and he* who *is held in* great respect 9 *dwells in it*'. [9]*Widows you sent away em*pty-handed.

VI

2 *ʾrḥk*: sing.; MT plural.
6 *ṣḥʾ*: participle peal.
7 By adding *wʾmrt* the targumist explains that the following words express Job's attitude as interpreted by Eliphaz.
9 *ryqnh* has adverbial force, cf. B-L, § 68p.

Column VII
(fragm. 6 left side; Job xxii 16-22)

1 [16]די מיתו] [17]
2 אמרין ל]אלהא
3 לנא אלה]א [18]
4 ועטת רש]יעין [19]
5 ויחאכון ו]
6 [20]היך לא]
7 [21]הסתכל]
8 [22]קבל]
9].

Column VIII
(fragm. 7; Job xxiv 12-17)

1 [12]מן קריהון]
2 תקבל אלהא] [13]
3 קדמוהי לנורה]
4 בשבילוהי [14]ל]
5 ומסכן ובלי]ליא [15]
6 קבל למא]מר
7 [16]ויחטאח]

VII

5 *wyḥ'kwn*: imperf. pael of *ḥwk*, cf. Jastrow *s.v.*

VIII

1 *qryhwn*: the suffix is not found in MT.

3 *qdmwhy*: before God?

7 *wyḥṭ'ḥ*[: we do not know for certain whether the ' (added afterwards above the line) belongs to the first or the second word. In the first case we have a form of *ḥṭ'*

COLUMN VII
Job xxii 16-22

1 [16]who died *untimely, whose foundation was flowing away like a river*; [17]*who* 2 said to *God*: '*Depart from us*! *what* 3 *can* God *do* for us?' [18]–*while it was He who filled their houses with good things.* 4 The counsel of the wic*ked is far from me!* [19]*The righteous see it* 5 and laugh, and *the innocent derides them.* 6 [20]How .... not .... 7 [21]Become wise .... 8 [22]Accept *instruction from his mouth* .... 9 ....

COLUMN VIII
Job xxiv 12-17

1 [12]From their cities *men groan, and the soul of the wounded* 2 cries: God *does not pay attention to what is absurd* [13]...................... 3 before Him in the fire; *they do not know his ways and do not stay* 4 in his paths. [14]Towards *day-break the murderer rises to slay the needy* 5 and the poor, and at nig*ht he becomes like a thief.* [15]*The eye of the adulterer waits for* 6 the dusk, think*ing*: '*No eye will see me!*' *He puts a cover over over his face* 7 [16]and in *the* d*ark* he breaks

« and he sins ». Here the second *ḥ* could be the initial letter of *ḥtr* (cf. MT); then the one verb of MT was rendered by two verbs in the targum. In the second case we have to think of the root *ḥṭṭ* « to dig », which corresponds exactly to *ḥtr* « to dig, to break into ». *ʾḥ*[then would be the beginning of *ʾḥšwkʾ* « in the dark », cf. *ʾbyt* = *bbyt* in 1QpHab XI, 6 and Murabbaʿat **42**, 4 (*DJD* II, Texte, p. 156); cf. for later Aramaic DALMAN, p. 229, who derives ʾ from *ʿl*.

בבאיש[17
להון[

Column IX
(fragm. 8; Job xxiv 24-xxvi 2)

(24) א/התכ]פפו כיבלא יתקפצון א[
25 מ]ן אפו יתיבנני פתגם וי.[
xxv 1 ענא בלד[ד
2 ש]לטן ורבו עם אלהא ע[בד
במרו]מה 3 האיתי רחצן להש[היה
] או על מן לא תקום [4
]אלהא ומא יצדק[5
] זכי וכוכביא לא[6
ב]ר אנש תולע[ה
xxvi 1 ענא איוב ואמ]ר 2 העד[רת

8 *bb'yš*[has no equivalent in MT. Perhaps *bb'yšthwn*.

IX

1 *ybl'* is the name of a plant (*cynodon dactylon* « Bermuda-grass »), cf. Jastrow *s.v.*; I. Löw, *Aramäische Pflanzennamen*, Leipzig, 1881, p. 183, and: *Die Flora der Juden* I, Wien, Leipzig, 1928 (reprint Hildesheim, 1967), pp. 697 f. MT reads *kl* which is probably also the name of a plant, cf. Löw, *Die Flora*... II, p. 231.

into houses, and by day they conceal themselves 8 in
their bad*ness; they do not know the light,* [17]*for* 9 to
them *morning is the same as darkness* ....
.....

Column IX
Job xxiv 24-xxvi 2

1 [(24)]........ they are be*nt down,* they shrink like
Bermuda-grass, *they wither like heads of grain.* 2
[25]*And if not, w*ho ever will give me an answer
and *turn my speech to nothing*? 3 [xxv] [1]Bilda*d the*
Shuhite began to speak 4 *and said*: [2]*Do*minion and
dignity are with God who m*akes peace* 5 *in* the *hig*h*est.*
[3]Is there any hope that He will de*lay* 6
.... or on whom does not rise ....
.....? [4]*How then can a man* 7 *be just before* God,
and how can be righteous *he that is born from a*
woman? [5]*Even the moon* 8 *is not* pure, nor the stars
clear in his sight. [6]*How much less man,* 9 *a maggot, the*
*s*on of man, a wor*m*! 10[xxvi 1] *Job began to speak*
*and sai*d: [2]Did *you* hel*p the powerless* ....
.......?

5 *rḥṣn lhš*[: here the targum deviates considerably from MT. The latter has: « Is there any numbering of his troops? » LXX, however, reads: « Let no one suppose that there will be delay for brigands ». Perhaps after *rḥṣn* the targum contained *lhšhyh,* inf. haphel of ***šhʾ*** « to delay ».

10 The targumist rendered *mèh* (MT) by *h- interrogativum,* probably in order to avoid the sarcasm of MT.

Column X
(fragm. 9; Job xxvi 10-xxvii 4)

[ע.] .[פי חסוך	10 1
י]זיע ויתמהון מן	11 2
]ימא ובמנדעה קטל	12 3
הד]נח חללת ידה תנין ערק	13 4
שבילו]הי מא עטר מלא נש]מע	14 5
מן]יסתכל	6
	7
ואמר ²חי אלהא]	xxvii 1 8
לנפשי ³הן לכמ]א	9
ב]אפי ⁴הן ימל]לן	10

Column XI
(fragm. 10 right side; Job xxvii 11-20)

בי]ד אלהא ועבד	11 (10) 1
כ]לכון חזיתון למה	12 2

X

1 It is impossible to supply with certainty the other letters
of the word preceding *ḥswk*. A possible conjecture is *ʿl*
(or *ʿm*) *sypy* « at the ends of », cf. TO Deut. iv 32. The
word *ḥswk* is a derivation from *ḥsk* « to withhold ». Perhaps the targumist considered MT *taklît* to derive from *klʾ*
« to withhold » (instead of *klh* « to be finished »).

2 *yzyʿ*: the targumist stresses God's sovereignty in making
Him the subject of the verb.

Column X
Job xxvi 10-xxvii 4

1 [10]*He marked a circle on the surface of the water* at the *en*ds (?) of the limit .... 2 [11]*The pillars of heaven He* causes to tremble, and they are stunned because of 3 *his rebuke.* [12]*By his power He tamed* the sea and by his knowledge He killed 4 *the serpent.* [13]*By his wind* He *brigh*tened *the sky*; his hand pierced the fleeting serpent. 5 [14]*Behold, these are* (*but*) *the fringe of* his *paths*; what a vague word we he*ar* 6 *of Him*! *But who* can understand *the thunder of his might*?

7

8 [xxvii 1]*Job continued his discourse* and said: [2]As God lives, *who withholds* 9 *my right, the Lord who has embittered* my soul: [3]verily, as long *as my spirit* 10 *is in me and the breath of God in* my nose, *my lips* wi*ll* not spea*k* 11 *falsehood.*

Column XI
Job xxvii 11-20

1[(10)] .... [11]*I will teach you about* God's *p*ower and the work of 2 *the Lord I will not*

5 Since the verb ‘ṭr (= Hebr. *qāṭar*) means « to smoke », the substantive ‘ṭr must denote « smoke, haze ».

9 *lkm’* is equivalent to *kl km’ d-* « as long as », cf. Jastrow, *s.v. km’*.

XI

1 ‘*bd* is a substantive (cf. also XXIII, 4; XXV, 2; XXVII, 3; XXVIII, 1; XXIX, 2).

3 [13]]אנש רשיען
4 מן]קדמוהי ינסון [14]הן
5 חר]ב יפצון ולא ישבעון
6 [15]]וארמלתה לא
7 [16]]זוזיא כטינא יסגא
8 [17] ומ]מ[ונ]ה קשיטה יפלג
9 [18]]..ן כקטותא
10 [19] יש]כב ולא איתחד
11 [20]]כמין באיש]תא

Column XII

(fragm. 10 left side and fragm. 11 right side; Job xxviii 4-13)

1 [(4)] רגל] [5] לח]ם
2 וחלי.] [6]את]רי
3 ספירא] [7]שביל]א
4 לא י]נדע [8]לא הד]רכה
5 תנין] [9] יד]ה

9 *qṭwt'* « branch » seems also to mean « cabin made of branches, booth ».

10 *'ytḥd*: for the preformative *'yt-* (instead of *'t*) cf. Murabba'at **18**, 2 (*DJD* II, Texte, p. 101). The subject of *'ytḥd* seems to be the wealth of the rich man.

conceal. 12*Behold, a*ll of you have seen it, why 3 *then do you speak vain things?* 13*This is* the wicked's *portion* 4 *from God, and the heritage which the tyrants* carry away *from* before Him: 14If 5 *his children increase, it is for the swor*d; they open (their) mouth, but they will not be satisfied 6 *with bread* 15..... ...., but his widows will not 7 *weep.* 16*Though he heaps up* money *like dust,* though he augments *cloths* 8 like mud,—17*he may augment (them) but the pious will wear them, and* the righteous will divide his *weal*th. 9 18*He builds his house like that of moth*s, like a booth 10 *made by a watchman.* 19*The rich man go*es to bed and nothing is taken away; 11 *he opens his eyes and all is gone.* 20Misfortun*es overtake him* like a flood,

Column XII
Job xxviii 4-13

(4)*forgotten by* 1 the foot *of man* .... 5*The earth—from it comes brea*d, 2 and change*d* .... 6*Pla*ces of 3 sapphire *are its stones, containing dust of gold.* 7The *path* 4 no *bird of prey knows, no vulture's eye has seen.* 8The serpent *has not* 5 *set* foot on it, *nor has the lion*

XII

2 *wḥly*[may be supplied with a *p* to make a peîl form of *ḥlp* « to exchange, to change », rendering MT *nèhpak.*

6 עק[ר 10 נהר]ין
7 ב[זע 11 יכ]לא
8 ו[12וחכמתא מן אן תשתכ]ח
9 [והיכא אתר ערימותא 13 אנ]ש

COLUMN XIII
(fragm. II left side; Job xxviii 20-28)

1 (20)אתר ערימותא 21 .[
2 צפרי שמיא אסת]תרת 22
3 באדנינא שמענא ש]מעה 23
4 בה ארו הוא ינד[ע(?) 24
5 לקצוי ארעא י.[
6 25 במעבדה לרוחא]
7 במכילה 26במעבד]ה
8 קלילין 27באדין[
9 28 ואמר לבני[אנשא
10 ומסטיא]

7 The verb *bzʿ* is commonly used in the targums to render MT *bqʿ*.

9 For the reconstruction of the text cf. XIII, 1 and XXXI, 2 (*hykʾ*).

XIII

2 *ʾsttrt*: ithpael (or ithpaal) of *str*.

4 *bh*: the preposition *b* suggests a form of *skl* (hithpaal) as

passed by it. [9]*He sets* his *hand to the rock,* 6 *he* uproots .... *the mountains.* [10]*In the rocks channels* 7 *he* hews *out, every precious thing his eye sees.* [11]*He brid*les *the sources of the rivers* 8 and *brings hidden things to light.* [12]*But wisdom, where can it be found*, 9 *and where ever is the place of understanding*? [13]*M*an *knows not the path to it.*

Column XIII
Job xxviii 20-28

[(20)]*and where ever is* 1 the place of understanding? [21]......................... *and from* 2 the birds of the sky *it* is hi*dden.* [22]*Perdition and death say*: 3 'With our ears we have heard a ru*mour of it*'. [23]*God understands* 4 it, since it is He who kno*ws its place.* [24]*For* 5 He *looks* to the ends of the earth, *He surveys everything under heaven.* 6 [25]When He made *a weight* for the wind *and meted out the waters* 7 by measure, [26]when *He* made *a law for the rain and a course for* the swift 8 *clouds,* [27]then *He saw it and appraised it, He established and fathomed it*; 9 [28]and He said to the sons of *man*: '*Behold, the fear of the Lord is wisdom,* 10 and to turn *from evil is understanding*'.

the preceding verb. For the rendering of MT *bîn* by *skl* cf. XXIX, 5 (Job xxxvii 14).

5 The *stat. constr.* plur. *qṣwy* is attested in Hebrew only (Psalm xlviii 11; lxv 6; Is. xxvi 15).

8 *qlylyn*: the targumist considered MT *qōlôt* « voices, sounds » to be the plur. fem. of the adjective *qal*.

10 *msṭy'*: *nomen actionis* from *sṭ'* « to go astray ».

Column XIV

(fragm. 12; Job xxix 7-16)

(7)ב]צפרין בתרעי קריא בשוק[א
[8]י]חזוני עלומין טשו וגברין ..[
[9]ו]רברבין חשו מללא וכף ישון[על פומהון
[10]קל[סגין הטמרו לחנך דב]ק לשנהון
[11]ת]שמע אדן שבחתני ועין ח[זת
[12]א]רו אנה שיזבת לענא מן .[
ד]י לא עדר להון [13]ברכת א[בד
בפ[ם ארמלה הוית לצלו]תא [14]
לבש]תני וככתון לבשת [[15]
ו]רגלין לחגיר [[16]
ל]א ידע[ת

Column XV

(fragm. 13; Job xxix 24-xxx 4)

(23) [24]אחאך להון ולא יה[ימנון

XIV

1 The word « morning » does not occur in MT, but LXX reads « at dawn » (ὄρθριος) instead of « gate », probably taking *šaʿar* as *šaḥar*. The targum preserved both traditions.

2 For the same syntactical construction (imperf. in the protasis and perfect in the apodosis) cf. line 5.
ʿlwm is equivalent to Hebr. *ʿèlèm* (segolate form); in

Column XIV
Job xxix 7-16

[7]*Every time I went out* 1 *in* the morning to the gates of the city, in *the* square *prepared my seat*—2 [8]*when* the youngsters saw me they hid and the men *rose to their feet and stood* 3 [9]*and* the chieftains stopped talking and put their hand *on their mouth*; 4 [10]the nobles suppressed their voice, and *their tongue* stuc*k* to their palate. 5 [11]*When* an ear heard (me) it praised me and when an eye s*aw* (*me*) *it gave witness to me.* 6 [12]*F*or I was it who rescued the miserable from *the mighty one, and the orphans* 7 *wh*o had no helper. [13]The blessing of the pe*rishing came upon me*; 8 *in the m*outh of the widow I was (the reason) for a pray*er.* [14]*Righteousness* 9 *cloth*ed itself with me and as with a tunic I clothed myself *with my justice.* [15]*I was eyes* 10 *to the blind and* feet to the lame. [16]*I was a father to the poor* 11 *and I investigated the case of him that I* did *no*t know.

Column XV
Job xxix 24-xxx 4

1 (23) . . . . [24]I smiled on them, but they did

Aramaic the stressed vowel normally occurs in the second syllable.
3 *yšwn*: imperf. pael 3rd pers. plur. of *šw*ʾ.
4 *ḥnk*: another instance of dissimilation (*ḥikkā*ʾ > *ḥinkā*ʾ).
7 ʿ*dr* and ʾ*bd* are participles.

XV

1 *yhymnwn*: imperf. haphel of ʾ*mn*.

2]ון [25]בחרת ארחי והוית ר]אש

3]בראש חילה וכגבר די א]בלין

4 [xxx 1]וכען ח]אכו עלי זערין מני ביומין[

5 אבה]תהון מלמהוא עם כלבי ע]ני [2]

6]לא הוא לי צבין ובאכפי]הון

7 [3] בכ]פן רעין הוא ירק ד]חשת

8]באישה [4]די אכל]ו

9 רתמ]ין לחמהו]ן [5]

Column XVI

(fragm. 14; Job xxx 13-20)

1 [(13)] לס]תרי יתון ופצא לא

2]ן [14]בתקף שחני יתון

3 תחות]באישה אתכפפת [15]התכפפת

4 עלי כ]רוח טבתי ורבותי וכענן

5 פורק]ני [16]וכען עלי תתאשד

2 *'rḥy*: MT has *darkām*.

5 *mlmhw'*: infinitive peal of *hw'* preceded by the prepositions *mn* and *l*.

6 *b'kpyhwn* « in their burdens ». MT reads *'ālêmô* « upon them ». Perhaps the translator understood this as *'ulēmô* « their yoke ».

7 *r'yn* could be the plural of *r'* « bad », but probably the substantive sing. *r'yn* « desire » is to be preferred. The text deviates considerably from MT.

dḥšt « desert » (the word is intact in XXXII, 5) originates

not be*lieve*, *nevertheless the light of my face* 2 they *did not cause to fall.* [25]I chose my way and was a ch*ief*; *I dwelt* 3 *as a king* at the head of his army and as a man that *comforts* mour*ners*. 4 [xxx 1]*But now* those who are younger in days than I *de*ride me, *wh*ose *father*s 5 *I would have disdained* being with the dogs of *my* flo*ck*. [2]*The strength of* 6 *their hands* was not a pleasure to me and in *their* burdens .... 7 [3]....... *in* (their) *hu*nger the vegetation of the de*sert* was their desire .... 8 .... bad ..... [4]Who at*e* .... 9 *and the root of broom*s was thei*r* bread [5]........

Column XVI
Job xxx 13-20

1[(13)]........... *in order to cause* my *ru*in they come, but *there is* nobody who saves 2 .... [14]Fervently my ulcers come out; 3 I am bent down *under* misfortune. [15]My prosperity has turned 4 *with me like* a wind, so did my dignity, yea like a cloud 5 my *welfa*re. [16]And now *my soul* is poured

from Persian. It was also adopted in Syriac, see Brockelmann, p. 169b.

XVI

1 *lstry* « for my ruin »; cf. Syriac *s^{e}tārā᾽* « destruction ».
2 *btqp* renders MT *k^{e}pèrèṣ* « as (through) a breach ». In Job xvi 14 *pèrèṣ* is rendered *tqwp* (Jastrow *s.v.*: « attack ») in tg 2.
šḥny: from *šḥn* « ulcer »; cf. Hebr. *š^{e}ḥîn*. The word occurs also in 4QOrNab and in tg 2, ii 7.

6 נפשי וי]ומי תשברא יאקפוני
7 [17]לילא מעלי] גרמי יקדון ועדק[י
8 [18]]חיל יאחדון לבו[שי
9 יתק]פוני [19]אחתוני ל[טינא
10 [20] ע]ליך].

Column XVII

(fragm. 15 right side; Job xxx 25-xxxi 1)

1 (24) [25]]אתה
2 [26]]בדי
3 [27] רת]חו ולא
4 [28]]הלכת
5]זעקת
6 [29] לבנ]ת יענה
7 [30]]ו מן
8 [31] אבוב[י
9 xxxi [1]]לא

6 *tšbr'*: this word may be connected with the root *šbr* « to suffer », occurring in an ossuary inscription from Jerusalem (see J. Naveh, The Ossuary Inscription from Giv'at ha-Mivtar, *Israel Exploration Journal* 20 (1970), pp. 33-37); cf. also *mšbr* in 1QHodayot III, 8.9, which may mean « pain ».
y'qpwny: imperf. aphel of *nqp*« to surround ».

out 6 within me *and d*ays of pain surround me. 7
[17]*By night* my bones burn *within me* and *my* tendons
8 *have no rest.* [18]*With great* force they grasp *my*
garme*nt*, 9 *like the collar of my tunic the*y *shu*t me in.
[19]They caused me to descend into *the mire* 10 . . . .
. . . . [20]*I cry* to you, *but you do not answer.*

Column XVII
Job xxx 25-xxxi 1

1 [(24)] . . . . [25] . . . .
. . . . . . 2 . . . . [26] . . . .
. . . . 3 . . . .
. . . . [27]*My bowels boi*l without 4 *ceasing* . . . .
. . . . [28]*In gloom* I
go about 5 *with no sun. I stand up in the assembly and*
cry. 6 [29] . . . . *and a*
*companion to the os*triches. 7 [30] . . . .
. . . . *and my bones are scorch*ed
by 8 *the heat* [31] . . . . , my *flute to the voice of*
weepers. 9 [xxxi 1] . . . . *that I*
would not *look upon a virgin.*

7 *yqdwn* is to be derived from *yqd* « to burn ».
ʿdqy: the verb *ʿdq* means « to be fastened »: *ʿdqy*, in parallelism with *grmy*, probably means « my tendons »; cf. LXX τὰ δὲ νεῦρά μου.
9 *ʾḥtwny*: 3rd pers. plur. perf. aphel of *nḥt* with suffix.

XVII

8 *ʾbwb* is the usual targumic translation of MT *ʿûgāb*.

Column XVIII

(fragm. 15 left side + fragm. 16 right side; Job xxxi 8-16)

1	(8)יאכ[ל	[9]הן פ]תיא
2	לבי בא[נתתא	אטמ]רת
3	[10]תטחן ל[	[11]ארו ד]נא רגז
4	והוא חטא[[12]	הי]א עד
5	אבדון ת[אכל	[13]]הן אתקצרת
6	בדין עב[די	[14]]מא אעבד
7	כדי יק[ום אלהא	[15]]ארו
8	עבד[	ח]ד [16]הן
9	אמ[נע	ועיני ארמלה]סיפת

Column XIX

(fragm. 16 left side + fragm. 17 right side; Job xxxi 26-32)

1	(26)דנח ולס[הרא [27]	ל]בי

XVIII

1 *pty'*: peîl of *pt'* « to be open, to be accessible to influences, to open, to entice ». The final ' is an orthographic peculiarity (cf. *šwy'* « he placed » in XXIX, 6 and XXXI, 2; *tbw'* « they returned » in XXXII, 3), which is also found elsewhere in the Qumran scrolls. Because « woman » is preceded by the preposition *b* we have to translate « if my heart has been enticed by a woman ».

Column XVIII
Job xxxi 8-16

[8]*may I sow and another* 1 ea*t* .... [9]*If* my heart has been 2 *en*ticed by a w*oman or if* I have *hi*dden *myself at my neighbour's door,* 3 [10]let *my wife* grind for *another.* [11]*For th*at is a cause for anger 4 and that is an iniquity .... [12]*For it is a fire tha*t 5 *devour*s to Perdition.......... .... [13]If I have been short-tempered 6 with regard to the claim of *my* sla*ve* .... [14]what shall I do 7 when *God* ar*ises*? .... [15]For 8 He who made *me in the belly, made him*; *the same* One *fashioned us in the womb.* [16]If 9 I re*fused any need of the poor, or made the widow's eyes* to pine,

Column XIX
Job xxxi 26-32

[26]*If I looked at the sun when* 1 it shone, or at the moo*n marching in splendour,* [27]*so that* my *hea*rt *was*

2 *ʾṭmrt*: ithpaal of *ṭmr* « to hide, to preserve, to guard ».
3 *tṭḥn*: the translator omitted the second part of the verse because he deemed its contents shocking. Apparently he did not interpret the verb *ṭḥn* (MT) in a sexual sense. For the sexual connotation of the verb cf. LXX; GenRabba 48 at xviii 12, and bSoṭah fol. 10a.
9 *sypt*: pael perf. 1st pers. sing. of *swp* (or aphel, if *ʾsypt* is to be read).

2 ונשקת ידי ל[פמי [28] כד]בת

3 לאלהא מעל[א [29] ה]ללת

4 על באישתה[ ].א

5 לוטי וישמע[ ]ברגזי

6 ואחדת א[[30] למחט]א

7 חכי למש[אל [31] א]נש

8 ביתי מ[ן [32]]

9 לא י[ ]

Column XX

(fragm. 17 left side; Job xxxi 40-xxxii 3)

1 [40]תחות חטא[

2 באשושה ספ[ו xxxii 1

3 אלין מלהתב[ה

4 הוא איוב ז[כי

5]

XIX

3 *hllt* « I exulted ». *hll* is not found in the Aramaic dictionaries, but it is attested in 1QGenAp XXI, 2. The LXX reads « he (or « I ») said », which would correspond to *mllt*.

4-6 As compared with MT the targumist enlarged the text considerably.

secretly seduced 2 and my hand kissed *my mouth,*
[28]*that also would have been an offence before the law, for*
I would have *l*ied 3 to God on hi*gh.* [29]*If I rejoiced*
*at my foe's misfortune and ex*ulted 4 because of his
trouble, ‹................................... 5 my
curse and he heard ....
.... in my anger 6 and I have taken ....
.............› [30]*Neither have I allowed* my palate
7 *to s*in by see*king his life with a curse.* [31]*Did not the*
*m*en of 8 my house *say*: 'Wh*o*.....................
......................?' [32]*In the street* 9 *the*
stranger did not *sleep* ....
....

Column XX

Job xxxi 40-xxxii 3

1 [40]Instead of wheat *let thistles grow, instead of barley,*
2 rue. *The words of Job are* ended. xxxii [1]*So* these
three men ceased 3 answeri*ng Job because* 4 Job was
ri*ghteous in his own eyes.* 5

XX

2 *b'šwšh* renders MT *bŏ'šāh* « weeds ». The Aramaic word denotes a plant with bitter strong-scented leaves, the *peganum harmala L.* « rue »; cf. I. Löw, *Aramäische Pflanzennamen*, Leipzig, 1881, p. 371, and *Die Flora der Juden* III, Wien/Leipzig, 1924 (reprint Hildesheim, 1967), pp. 507 f.; also Brockelmann, p. 98b.

[2]אדין רגז]
זרע רומא]ה
[3]ואף ע]ל
מלי]ן

Column XXI
(fragm. 18; Job xxxii 10-17)

(10)מלי אף אנה [11]ארו סברת]
תסיפון עד תחקרון סוף[[12]
וארו לא איתי מנכון לא]יוב
למלוהי [13]די למה תאמרון]
להן אלהא חיבנא ולא א]נש [14]
מלין וכמא לא יתיבנה] [15]
והחשיו ונטרת מנהון [[16]
קמו ולא ימללון עו]ד [17]
וא]חוה מלי אף א]נה [18]

6 *rgz* seems to be a verb. The usual targumic translation of MT *ḥārāh ʾap* is *tqp rgz*, cf. II, 1.
7 *rwmʾh*: a town called *rûmāh* is mentioned in 2 Ki. xxiii 36, cf. Josephus BJ iii, 233.

XXI

4 *dy lmh tʾmrwn* « lest you should say » i.e. « do not say », cf. TJ Is. xxxvi 18.

6 [2]Then grew angry *Elihu, son of Barachel the Buzite of* 7 the family of Rum*a* .... 8 [3]And also ag*ainst his three friends his anger flared up because they had not found* 9 words ....
....

Column XXI
Job xxxii 10-17

[10]*So I say*: *listen to me,* 1 I too *will display* my words. [11]Behold, I waited for *your words, I gave ear till* 2 you had finished, till you had searched out the final end. [12]*I paid close attention to you* 3 but behold, J*ob* has nobody among you *who gave answer to* 4 his words. [13]Do not say: '*We have found wisdom*! 5 But it is God who blames us and not a m*an*'. [14]*He has not stringed together* 6 words *against me*; nobody at all answers him .... [15]*They are dismayed* 7 and they keep silent, and *speech* **is** withheld from them. [16]*Am I to wait because they do* **not** *speak, because* 8 they stand there and do not speak a**ny** mo*re*? [17]*I will also take part in the discussion*; 9 I too will *di*splay my words [18]..................... ....

2 *swp* probably renders MT *millîn*.
6 *ytybnh*: MT has the 1st pers. « I shall (not) answer him ». In MT a word corresponding to *wkm'* is lacking.
7 *nṭrt* seems to be a peîl form with 3rd pers. fem. ending; cf. B-L, § 80.

Column XXII

(fragm. 19; Job xxxiii 6-16)

1 [(6)]אנ]ה [7]הן חרגתי לא תסר[דנך
2 יי]קר [8]הך אמרת באדני וק[ל
3 [9]זכ]י אנה ולא חטא לי ונקא[
4 [10]ה]ן עולין השכח אחד לי [
5 [11]י]שוא בסדא רגלי וסכר כ[ל
6 [12b]ארו רב אלהא מן אנשא[[13]
7 רבברן תמלל ארו בכל פ[תגמוהי
8 [14]א]רו בחדא ימלל אלה[א
9 [15]ב]חלמין בהדידי ליילא[
10 בניו]מה על משכבה[[16]
11].רה[

Column XXIII

(fragm. 20+21 right side+fragm. A4; Job xxxiii 24-32)

1 [(24)]ויאמר פצהי מן חב[לא [(25)]]ת

XXII

1 *tsrdnk*: the restoration is based on the Syriac verb *srd*: pael « to dismay, to frighten ».

2 Though *hk* may mean « how », which, however, is written *plene* elsewhere in the text (*hyk*, VII, 6), here the interpretation taking it as an equivalent to Hebr. *ʾak* « surely » is to be preferred.

5 *wskr*: this reading (« and he blocks up ») is preferable to *wsbr* (cf. Hebr. *śābar* in Neh. ii 13.15 « to inspect »).

6 The targumist left out vs. 12a.

7 *rbbrn,* instead of *rbrbn,* is a slip of the pen. For the expres-

Column XXII
Job xxxiii 6-16

[(6)]*I have been nipped from clay*, 1 I *too*. [7]Indeed, fear
of me should not frig*hten you, nor should my pressure*
2 *be too he*avy *on you*. [8]*Surely*, you have said in my
ears, and *I have heard* the so*und of your words*: 3
[9]'I am *pu*re and have no sin, *I am* innocent *and have*
no guilt. 4 [10]*Ye*t He found transgressions, seized me,
counted me his enemy. 5 [11]*He* puts my feet in the stocks
and He blocks up al*l my paths*'. 6 [12b]Seeing that God
is greater than man, [13]*why* do you speak *against Him*
7 proud words? For *He gives no account* of any *of his*
a*cts*. 8 [14]*In*deed, Go*d* may speak in one way *or*
another—one does not perceive it: 9 [15]*in* dreams, during
the night, *when deep sleep falls upon men*, 10 *in*
*slumb*ers, upon the bed [16]. 11
. . . .

Column XXIII
Job xxxiii 24-32

[24]*And He will have pity on him* 1 and He will say:

sion see Dan. vii 8.20 and cf. Apocal. xiii 5; Ass. Mosis vii 9 « os eorum loquetur ingentia ».

9 *bhdydy* « during the time of », cf. Jastrow s.v. *hd-*.

XXIII

1 *pṣhy* « deliver him ». The suffix *-hy*, instead of *-hw*, is found after various verbal forms: *bnhy* (perf.) Ezra v 11; TJ 1 Ki. vi 38; *rmyhy* (imper.) TO Ex. iv 3; TJ 2 Ki. ix 26; *hbhy* (imper. fem.) Cowley 13, 16; *hḥsnhy* (imper. fem.) Cowley 8, 26; cf. B-L, §§ 38w; 47n; Leander *ÄgAr*, §§ 31f.h; 32g; 38d, and not only after forms ending in *-w* (B-L, § 13q).

2 אשה ישנקנה ויתמלין [ ]מן

3 עולים ותב ליומי עלימ[ותה [26] ו]ישמענה

4 ויחזא אנפוהי באסי[ותא] וכעבד

5 כפוהי [י]שלם לה [27]ויאמ[ר]ולא

6 כארחי ה[ש]תלמת [28]פר[ק]ה

7 בנהור תחזא [29]הא [ג]בר

8 זמן תרין תלתה [30]לא[תבה בנהו]ר

9 חי[י]ן [31]הצת דא [אמ]לל

10 [32][הן א]יתי מ[לין]

2 *ʾšh* « fire ». This would fit in very well with *yšnqnh* « will choke him ». *ʾšh,* however, is fem. and the preceding word, which ends in *t,* also seems to be a fem. (in the construct state). In addition, the idea of being choked does not go well with the idea of being delivered (line 1). So there may have been a negation in the lacuna of line 1, and *ḥblʾ* may be the implied subject of *yšnqnh*. Since *ḥblʾ* here denotes destruction in Sheol *ʾšh* probably indicates the infernal fire. If this is right the *t* might be the final letter of *ymt,* st. cstr. of *ymh* « sea, lake », which in Pesh Apocal. xx 14.15 (Greek λίμνη) denotes the abyss (of fire). So the Job targum may have read something like « lest it (i.e. destruction) chokes him in the abyss of fire ».

'Deliver him from destru*ction* ...‹..............
of 2 fire it chokes him'. Then *his bones* will be filled
with *marrow*›, [25]*his flesh will be fresh*er than 3 that
of a boy, and he returns to the days of *his* you*th*.
[26]*He prays to God and* He hears him, 4 and in regaining
he*alth* he will see his face .... and
according to the work of 5 his hands *He will* requite
him. [27]And he will sa*y*: 'I *have sinned and perverted
what is right*, but I have not 6 been *re*quited according
to my way'. [28]He has deli*vered his soul from going
down to the Pit and* his *life* 7 sees the light. [29]Behold,
*all these things God does with a m*an, 8 (even) twice or
thrice, [30]tu*rn*ing *back his soul from the Pit, that
he may be enlightened with the li*ght of 9 li*f*e. [31]Heed
this, *Job, listen to me*; *be silent, and I will s*p*eak*. 10
[32]*If the*re are wo*rds, answer me* ....
....

yšnqnh: the targumist presumably gave a double translation of the text, according to the two possibilities of the (unvocalized) Hebrew: 1) *yšnqnh* « strangles, chokes him » may render MT *mnʿr*, considered to be the part. piel of *nʿr* « to drive, to push, to pull », occurring in Ex. xiv 27, where TO renders *šnyq* (pael); 2) he translated *mnʿr* by *mn ʿwlym* (ll. 2/3).
wytmlyn: 3rd pers. plur. fem. ithpeel of *mlʾ*. The LXX also has the verb « to fill »: « he will fill his bones with marrow ».

8 *zmn tryn* « twice ». Cf. Dalman, pp. 133-135, where similar expressions are given.

9 *hṣt*: imper. haphel of *ṣwt*.

Column XXIV

(fragm. 21 left side + fragm. 22; Job xxxiv 6-17)

1 [6]מן חטא [7]מ]ן]א חטיא [8]ומתחבר

2 לעבדי שקר] רש]ע [9]ארו אמר לא

3 ישנא גבר מי] ב]תר אלהא

4 [10]כען אנש]]חס לאלהא מן שקר

5 ומן לחבלא מ]רא [11]]אנש ישלם לה

6 ////////////] [12]]הכען צדא אלהא

7 ישקר ומרא] [13]]הוא ארעא עבד

8 וקשט תב]ל [14] נשמ]תה עלוהי יכלא

9 [15]וימות [ ] ישכבון

10 [16]] מ]לי [17]הבשקר

Column XXV

(fragm. 23; Job xxxiv 24-34)

1 [24] ר]ברבין די לא סוף ויקים א]חרנין

2 [25a] יחכ]ם עבדהון [26aβ]וירמא המון באת]ר

XXIV

1 *ḥṭy'*: probably sing.

2 *šqr*: on the strength of the Hebrew *Vorlage* and the synonyms used in this column *šqr* has obviously the comprehensive meaning « evil, iniquity ».

3 *yšn'* « he does (not) change ». MT reads « he has no profit ».

Column XXIV
Job xxxiv 6-17

'... [6]*In spite of my right I am called a liar. My wound is incurable* 1 though I am without sin'. [7]Wh*o is a man like Job who drin*ks sin *like water* [8]and keeps company 2 with evildoers, *consorting with men of wick*edness? [9]For he says: 'Not 3 does a man change by .... *af*ter God'. 4 [10]Now, you men *of good sense, listen to me*: far be it from God (to do) evil, 5 and from the Lo*rd* to injure. [11]*But the work of* a man He shall requite him 6

.... [12]Now then, will God really
7 do evil and the Lord *pervert justice*? [13]It is He who made the earth 8 and prepared *the whole* worl*d*. [14]*If* .... He withdrew to Himself his *spirit and brea*th, 8 [15]*all flesh* would die *together, and men* would lie down *in the dust.* 10 [16]*Now, if you have understanding, hear this, give ear to the sound of* my *wo*rds. [17]Is it by injustice

Column XXV
Job xxxiv 24-34

1 .... [24]*He shatters the m*ighty without limitation and sets o*thers* 2 *in their stead.* [25a]*Because He kno*ws

The translator may have deemed this expression disrespectful.

6 *ṣdʾ* « indeed, really », cf. Dan. iii 14.

XXV

2 The targumist left out Job xxxiv 25b and the beginning of verse 26.

3 [27] אר]חה ובכל שבילוהי לא הסתכ[לו

4 [28]]מסכנין וקבילת ענין ישמע [[29]

5 ויסת]ר אנפוהי מן יתיבנה על עם[

6 [30] ממ]לך אנש רשיעיא התקלו [

7 [31]]תי לה איחל [32] בלחודוהי[אחזא

8]לא אוסף [33]ארו מ.[

9 אנתה תב]חר ולא אנה [

10 [34] מ]לין וגבר[

Column XXVI

(fragm. 24 + fragm. 25 right side; Job xxxv 6-15)

1 [(6)]בך ובסגיא עויתך מא ת[עבד לך(?) [7]הן זכי]ת מא

3 MT *mēʾaḥ*^{a}*râw* « from after him » has been rendered [*mn*] *ʾrḥh*, cf. LXX.

6 If the reading *mmlk* is correct it must be an inf. peal. The construction is rather obscure, cf. also MT.
htqlw: hithpaal of *tql* « to stumble, to be ensnared ». MT reads a plural participle: « ensnarers » (of the people).

7 *-ty*: if this reading is correct it must be assumed that the text contained a fem. subst. with suffix 1st pers. sing. instead of a verbal form (MT).
ʾyḥl « I will wait, hope for ». The verb is not attested in the Aramaic dictionaries.

their work [26aβ]He throws them down in the pla*ce of* .... 3 [27]............. *from* his *way* and did not he*ed* any of his paths, 4 [28]*to bring before Him the cry of* the poor, so that He hears the plaint of the wretched [29]*When* 5 *He keeps quiet, who can condemn, and when He hid*es his face, who can answer Him – with respect to a nation *or to* 6 *a man equally* [30]....... *the ru*le of the wicked; they have been ensnared .... 7 [31]‘.................... my ...., for Him I wait, [32]at Him only *I look.* 8 *Be you my teacher*: *if I have done evil,* I will not continue’. [33]Behold .... 9 .... *for it is you who de*cide, not me; *therefore tell what* 10 *you know.* [34]*Men of good sense will speak* words *to me,* and the *wise* man *who hears me*:

Column XXVI
Job xxxv 6-15

[6]*If you have sinned what can you do* 1 by yourself, and if your iniquities are a multitude what *can* you *do*

blḥwdwhy « at him only ». MT reads *bilʿadēy* « without, apart from ».

XXVI

1 *bk*: MT has the suffix of the 3rd pers. masc. sing. According to *bk* we propose to supply *lk* instead of *lh* (MT *lô*) in the lacuna.
*sgy*ʾ is used as a substantive, cf. line 3; XXVIII, 4 and Aḥiqar, 106.

2 תתן לה או מא מידך יקבל[[8]לגבר כות]ך
חטיך
3 ולבר אנש צדקתך [9]מן סגיא[יז]עקון
יצוחון
4 מן קדם סגיאין [10]ולא אמר[ין]אלהא
5 די עבדנה ודי חלק לנא ל[שן מזמ]ר לנצבתנא
6 בליליא [11]די פרשנא מן בע[ירי ארעא ומן]
צפריא
7 חכמנה [12]תמה יזעקון ול[א יענה מן קדם ג]אות
8 ב]אישין [13]ארו שוא יש]מע אלהא ומרא ה]בלא
9 לא] יצתנה [14]הן תאמר[ ]
10]. לה [15]א]רו [

Column XXVII

(fragm. 25 left side + fragm. 26 right side; Job xxxvi 7-16)

1 [(7)]למלכין יתבי כ[ורסיהון ור]חמוהי לרחצן ירמון

5 *lšn mzmr*: if we correctly supplied the text the targumist seems to have rendered MT *z^e^mirôth* according to its twofold connotation (« praise »; « strength »).
lnṣbtn': the meaning of *niṣb^e^tā'* in Dan. ii 41 « firmness » pleads in favour of the translation « for our steadfastness » instead of « for our plantation », which seems to be less probable here.

6 *pršn'*: the targumist seems to have read the part. hiphil of *pālāh* instead of the part. piel of *'ālap*.

7 Here *tmh* seems to be a conjunction introducing a conditional phrase.

for yourself? [7]*If* you *are righteous* what 2 do you give Him or what does He receive from your hand? [8]Your sin *concerns a man like* yourself 3 and your righteousness a son of man. [9]On account of the multitude of *oppressions* they *ca*ll for help, they cry out 4 because of so many. [10]But *they* do not say: '*Where is* God 5 who made us, who granted us *a prai*sing to*ngue* (?) for our steadfastness 6 during the night, [11]who distinguished us from the be*asts of the earth and more than* the birds 7 made us wise?' [12]When they call for help, *He does* no*t answer, because of the pr*ide of 8 *ev*il men. [13]Behold, *God* hea*rs* vanity, *but* of *fu*tility *the Lord* 9 *does not* take notice. [14]If you say .... 10 .... for Him. [15]Be*hold*,...................... ....

Column XXVII
Job xxxvi 7-16

1 [(7)]kings who sit on *their* thr*one, and* his *fr*iends will

8 *ʾrw*: this particle introduces a phrase which in MT is an interrogative sentence, as in XVIII, 7 (xxxi 15) and XXV, 8 (xxxiv 33); it obviously means « behold ».

XXVII

1 In *lmlkyn*, which renders MT *ʾèt mᵉlākîm*, the preposition probably denotes an accusative.
lrḥṣn is the common targumic rendering of Hebr. *lābèṭaḥ*, e.g. TO Lev. xxv 18.19 and Deut. xxxiii 12.
yrmwn is written defectively (from *rwm* « to be high »).

2 [8]ואף עם אסירין ב[זיקין א]חידין בחבלי מסכניא

3 [9]ויחוא להון עבדיהו[ן ועוית]הון ארו התרוממו [10]ויגלא

4 אדניהון למוסר וא[מר להון]הן יתובון מן באישתהון

5 [11]הן ישמעון ויעב[דון ישלמון]בטב ימהון ושניהון

6 ביקר ועדנין [12][והן לא ישמ]עון בחרבא יפלון

7 ויאבדון מן מ[נדעא [13] ל]בבהון לרגז

8 עליהון .[[14] מ]דינתהון בממתין

9 [15]ויפרק מ[סכנא]די אדניהון

10 [16]]]לא[ ]

Column XXVIII

(fragm. 26 left side + fragm. 27; Job xxxvi 23-33)

1 [(23)]ע[ולא עבדת [24]ד]כר ארו רברבין עבדוהי ד[י אנש

2 חזוה[ון [25]וכ]ל אנשא עלוהי חזין ובני אנשא

3 מרחיק [ב]ה יבקון [26]הא אלהא רב הוא ויומוהי

2 *ʿm*: MT reads *ʾim*.
4 *mwsr* « discipline » seems to be a Hebrew loan-word.
5 *ymhwn* is written defectively (for *ywmyhwn*).
8 *mmtyn*: MT reads *qᵉdēšîm* « male prostitutes ». *mmtyn* is either the active or the passive participle aphel of *myt*. Seeing that LXX translates « angels » (of vengeance), probably reading *qᵉdōšîm*, and seeing that in Job xxxiii

be exalted in safety. 2 [8]And this also goes for those
who are fettered in *chains, h*eld in the cords of the
wretched: 3 [9]He shows them thei*r* works *and* their
iniquities, that they exalted themselves, [10]and He
opens 4 their ears to discipline, and sa*ys to them*:
'If they turn from their evil, 5 [11]if they obey and
ac*t* (accordingly), *they shall spend* their days in
prosperity and their years 6 in dignity and felicity;
[12]*but if t*hey *do not ob*ey, they shall fall by the sword, 7
and they shall perish without kn*owledge*' [13]........
.... their *he*art for anger 8 upon them ....
.... [14] .... their *dwe*lling-place with the
slayers. 9 [15]But He delivers the w*retched* ....
.... of their ears. 10 [16]..............
.... not ......

Column XXVIII
Job xxxvi 23-33

[23]*Who has prescribed for Him his way, and who has
said*: 1 '*you have done* wro*ng*'? [24]*Re*member that very
great are his works, wh*ich men* 2 have seen; [25]*and
eve*ry man looks to Him and the sons of man 3 from
afar inquire *after* Him. [26]Lo, God is great and his

22 the Masoretes vocalized *mmtym* as an active participle (LXX: ἐν ᾅδῃ), we prefer to take *mmtyn* in the same sense.

XXVIII

2 *ḥzw(hwn)* renders MT *šōr^{e}rû* which the targumist derived from the root *šûr* « to see ».

4 סגיא] לא נ]דע ומנין שנוהי די לא סוף [27]ארו

5 עננ]ין]וזיקי מטר יהכן [28]ועננוהי ינחתון

6 ט]יפין על]עם סגיא [29]הן מן פרס

7 ע]נני אתרגו]שתה מן טלל[30]ופרס נה]ורה

8] כ]סי [31]ארו בהון ידין ע]ממין

9] [32]על מאמרה מ]

10 [33]י]שיח על]והי

Column XXIX

(first column of the small scroll + fragm. B and C; Job xxxvii 10-19)

1 (10)על אנפי מין [11]אף בהון ימרק עננ]ין] וינפק מן

2 ענן נורה [12]והוא אמר ישמעון לה ואזלין לעבדיהון

3 על כל די ברא יפקדנון על אנפי תבל [13]הן למכתש

4 הן לארעא הן לכפן וחסרנה והן פתגם טב להווא

4 *sgy'* is used as a substantive, cf. XXVI, 1.3.

5 *yhkn*: imperf. haphel of *kwn* (cf. Syriac).

7 The conjecture *'trgwšth* is based on the fact that MT *t^ešu'ôt* is so rendered in TJ Is. xxii 2 and tg 2 Job xxxix 7. If our reading is correct *mn ṭll* must be read *min ṭ^elal* which corresponds to MT *sukkātô*. For *ṭll* corresponding to *sukkāh* cf. Jastrow s.v.

days 4 are numerous – *we do not* know (them), nor the number of his endless years. [27]Behold, 5 .... *the* clouds, and He prepares the rain-winds. [28]And his clouds let 6 d*rops* come down *upon* a numerous people. [29]Behold, who spreads out 7 his *thund*er-c*louds* from (their) pavilion, [30]and spreads out *his* ligh*tning* 8 *upon them and* covers *the roots of the sea*? [31]For by them He judges pe*oples* 9 .... [32]At his command .... 10 .... [33]... speaks about *Him* ....

Column XXIX
Job xxxvii 10-19

[10]*With his winds God produces ice* 1 on the surface of the water. [11]Moreover, with them He brightens the cloud*s*, and sends from 2 the sky his fire. [12]And when He speaks they obey Him and set out for their chores. 3 Over all things He created He appoints them on the face of the earth: [13]either to batter 4 or to shatter or to (cause) famine and penury or to bring

XXIX

1 *bhwn* obviously refers to the divine forces, wind etc., which according to the preceding verse produce the ice (see MT).

3 *mktš* is rather the infin. of *ktš* than a substantive.

4 *l'r*ʿʾ renders MT *le'arṣô*, which does not make sense in the context. The form ʾ*r*ʿʾ must be taken as the inf. aphel of *r*ʿʿ « to break, to shatter ».

5 עליה [14]הצת דא איוב וקום הסתכל בגבורת אלהא

6 [15]הת]נדע מא שויא אלהא עליהו[ן והו]פע נהור עננה

7 [16]התנ]דע להלבשא עננה גב[ורתא [17]ב]דיל די לבושך

8] [[16bβ]ארו הוא ידע מדע[א [18]]נפח ערפלא

9] כמח]זיה עקה [19]ינדע[ ]לנ[ ] [

Column XXX

(second column of the small scroll + fragm. D; Job xxxviii 3-13)

1 [3]אסר נא כגבר חל[ציך ואש]אלנך והתיבני //////// פתגם

2 [4]אן הוית במעבדי ארעא החויני הן ידעת חכמה

3 [5]מן שם משחתה הן תנדע מן נגד עליה חוטא [6]או

4 על מא אשיה אחידין או מן הקים אבן חזיתה [7]במזהר

5 כחדא כוכבי צפר ויזעק[ו]ן כחדה כל מלאכי אלהא

5 *ʿlyh* « on it », i.e. on the earth (*tbl*).

7/8 The text of these lines deviates from MT.

9 *ʿqh*: partic. fem. of *ʿwq* « to be pressed », Hebr. *ṣwq*, which the targumist seems to have connected with *mûṣāq*.

XXX

4 *ḥzyt* literally means « cutting, rough side of a stone ».

about something favourable 5 on it. [14]Listen to this, Job, come, and consider the mighty acts of God. 6 [15]*Do you* know how God commands the*m and causes* the light of his cloud to shine? 7 [16]*Do you k*now how to clothe his cloud with mig*ht*? [17]*Be*cause your garment 8 .... [16bβ]Behold, it is He who has knowledge. [18]*Do you know how to* inflate the dark sky 9 .... *like* a smooth *mir*ror? [19]He knows
•..............................

Column XXX
Job xxxviii 3-13

1 [3]Gird up *your* loi*ns* like a man, *that I may a*sk you, so give me an answer. 2 [4]Where were you when I made the earth? Tell me if you have wisdom! 3 [5]Who laid down its measures, if you know? **Who** stretched the line over it, [6]or 4 where are its ba**ses** fastened on, or who erected its **foundation-stone,** [7]when shone 5 together the morning stars and exult*ed*

Here *ʾbn ḥzyt* obviously refers to the rough stones in the foundation.
mzhr: inf. of *zhr* « to shine ». For theological reasons the targumist altered the text by changing MT « when sung » into « when shone ».

5 For similar reasons his text reads « angels of God » instead of « sons of God » (MT).

6 [8]התסוג בדשין ימא ב[הנ]גחותה מן רחם תהומא
7 למפק [9]בשוית ענין [לבו]שה וערפלין חותלוהי [10]ותשוה
8 לה תחומין ודת[ ]ין ו[ ]. [11]ואמרת עד תנא
9 ולא תוסף[ג]לל[יך] [12]הביומיך מנית
10 [13]]כנפ[י]אר[עא]

Column XXXI

(third column of the small scroll + fragm. E; Job xxxviii 23-34)

1 [23]ד[י ל]עדן ע[קת]א ליום קרב ואשתדו[ר[24]
2 היכא יפק ///////// ותשוב קדמוהי על ארעא [25]מן שויא
3 למטרא זמן וארח לענין קלילין [26]להנחתה על ארע
4 מדבר די לא אנש בה [27]להסבעה שיתא ושביקה

6-8 In lines 6-8 the forms of the finite verb differ from those in MT.

7 *bšwyt*: inf. constr. pael of *šwʾ* « to place », with the preposition *b*.

8 We propose to read [*ngr*]*yn w*[*dšyn*] in the lacuna.

XXXI

2 *tšwb* (from *nšb*) *qdmwhy*. The interpretation of *qdmwhy* meaning « his east winds » (from *qiddûm*, cf. TO Gen. xli 6, cf. also MT) is to be preferred to « before it ».

together all the angels of God? 6 [8]Did you shut the sea with doors when it *bro*ke forth from the womb of the depth 7 to find its way out, [9]when He made the clouds its *garm*ent and the dark clouds its swaddling bands? [10]Did you set 8 it bounds and law, *and fix it bar*s and *doors*? [11]Did you say: 'Thus far, 9 and no further; *here your proud* waves *shall halt*'? [12]Have you, in your days, ever commanded 10 *the morning, caused the dawn to know its place*? [13]............... *the* fringe*s of the* ear*th*?

Column XXXI
Job xxxviii 23-34

1 [23]wh*ich I have reserved for* the time of dis*tre*ss, for the day of war and battl*e*? [24]......... 2 where does it go out, and do you blow his east winds over the earth? [25]Who set 3 a time for the rain, and a way for the swift clouds, [26]to cause (them) to descend on a land of 4 wilderness, where there is no man,

3 *qōlôth* « sounds, voices » is once more rendered by *qlylyn* « swift », cf. XIII, 8.

4 *šytʾ wšbyqh*: MT *šōʾāh ûm*^{e}*šōʾāh* « wilderness and desert ». The targumist had in mind what grows in the desert: *šytʾ* « wild fig-tree » (Jastrow s.v.), « thorn-bush » (Sefire II A 5); *šbyqh* (or *šbwqh*?) = *šbqʾ* « undressed vine, isolated root » (in Syriac *šabbûqāʾ*) or = *šbyq* « spontaneous growth » with emphatic *h* (for both words cf. Jastrow).

5 ולהנפקה צמחי דתאה [28]האיתי למטרא אב או מן
6 ילד [ע]נני טלא [29]ומן בטן מן נפק גלידא
ושיקו[ע שמיא
7 מ[ן ילד]ה [30]כא[בן] מין התקרמו מנה ואנפי
תה[ומא
8 [31][ ]ע.[ ]כימא או סיג נפילא ת[
9 [32][ ]...א על בניה תיאש[[33]
10 [[34]]ענ[ין

Column XXXII

(fourth column of the small scroll + fragm. F; Job xxxix 1-11)

1 [(1)]יעלי כפא וחב[ל [2] י]רחיהין
2 שלמין ותנדע עדן מולדהין [3]ילדן בניהן ויפלטן
3 וחבליהן תושר [4]יקשן בניהן ויפקן נפקו ולא
תבוא

7 *mnh* « by it » i.e. « by the ice ». An equivalent is lacking in MT.

9 *ʿl bnyh*: before these words MT has *ʿayiš*, probably « the Great Bear »; though traces of letters are still visible we are unable to supply the corresponding word.

XXXII

3 *ḥblyhn* is literally « their throes of birth » but here it indicates what is brought forth by the throes, i.e. « their progeny », cf. the parallelism between *yaldēhèn* and *ḥèblēhèm* in MT.

twšr, aphel of *yšr*, here means « you send (out) », cf.

[27]to sate thorn-bush and wild growth 5 and to cause the shoots of plants to sprout? [28]Does the rain have a father, or who 6 begot the dew-*c*louds? [29]From whose womb came the ice, and the hoarfro*st of heaven* 7 who *bore* it? [30]As with sto*ne* the waters are covered by it and the surface of *the* flo*od is closed.* 8 [31]*Can you tie the fetters of* the Pleiades or *open* the fence of Orion? 9 [32]...................., can you relax the .... over its young [33].......... 10 ....[34]...... the cloud*s* ....

Column XXXII
Job xxxix 1-11

[1]*Do you know the birth season of* 1 the mountain-goats and *do you watch the* thro*es of the hinds*? [2]*Do you count* their *mo*nths 2 in full and do you know the time they bring forth? [3]When they bring forth their young and usher them into the world, 3 do you send forth their

Driver iii, 1; v, 1; ix, 3; xiii, 1.2, where the aphel is used of dispatching greetings and messages by letter, and of dispatching men carrying sculptures; cf. also papyrus xiii in the Brooklyn Aramaic Papyri (ed. by E. G. Kraeling, New Haven, 1935), and several occurrences in the Aramaic letters from Hermopolis (ed. by E. Bresciani and M. Kamil, Rome, 1966). In MT it is said that the animals « send out » their progeny.
tbwʾ « they return ». The final ʾ is an orthographic peculiarity, cf. XVIII, 1; XXIX, 6; XXXI, 2; 1QpHab II, 6 *yʾmynwʾ*; 1QGenAp XIX, 24; XXI, 26.28; XXII, 9 *hwwʾ*.

4 עליהן [5]מן שלח פראה ברחרין וחנקי ערדא מן
5 שרא [6]די שוית דחשת ביתה ומדרה בארע
מליחה
6 [7]וחאך על מהמא תקף קריא ונגשת שליט לא
7 ישמע [8]ויבחר לה טורין למ.[ו]בתר כל ירוק
8 ירדף [9]היבא ראמ[א ל]מפלחך או היבית על
9 אוריך [10]התקטר [ראמא ב]תוריה וילג[ן]
בבקעה
10 בת]ריך ות.[[11]התרחץ ב[ה ארו]
סגיא

Column XXXIII

(fifth column of the small scroll + fragm. I; Job xxxix 20-29)

1][20]התזיענה בתקף[
2 בסחרוהי אימה ודחלה [21]וחפר בבקע וירוט
ויחדא

5 *dḥšt*: cf. XV, 7.

6 *tqp* « strength » also includes other concepts in which the idea of strength is present, e.g. « anger ». The verb means « to be strong, heavy, vehement, hot, excited, sour ». Here the substantive obviously has the meaning « noise ».
ngśt: St. constr. of *ngśh* from the root *ngś* « to drive, prompt », hitherto not attested in Aramaic.

8 *hyb'*: imperf. of *'b'* « to be willing », with interrogative *h*.

9 *ylgn*: though the verb is not mentioned in the dictionaries, the substantives *lgn* « narrow path between fields » and

progeny? [4]They rear their young and send them out;
when they have left they do not return 4 to them.
[5]Who set the wild ass free and the bonds of the
onager, who 5 untied them, [6]whose home I made the
wilderness and whose dwelling (I made) in salt land?
6 [7]He laughs at the tumult, the noise of the city, and
the prompting of the driver he does not 7 hear.
[8]He chooses for himself the mountains as *his* pas*ture*
and after anything green 8 he hunts. [9]Will *the*
buffalo be willing *to* serve you, or will he reside at
9 your manger? [10]Can you tie *the buffalo with* ropes
and will he *draw* furrows in the valley 10 *aft*er you
and can you ....? [11]Can you rely on
him because great is 11 *his strength*?

Column XXXIII
Job xxxix 20-29

1 .... [20]Can you make
him leap with strength ....? 2 By his neighing
(he causes) fright and fear; [21]he paws in the valley,

lgnh « narrow path, row, bed » are to be found (see e.g. Jastrow).

XXXIII

2 *bsḥrwhy*: the substantive *sḥr* meaning « neighing » so far is not attested in Aramaic; in Arabic, however, there is a word *šaḫirun* which means « neighing » and obviously belongs to the same root.
yrwṭ derives from *rwṭ* (= *rhṭ* = Hebr. *rwṣ* « to run »), cf. 1QGenAp II, 19.

3 ובחיל ינפק לאנפי חרב [22]יחאך על דחלה ולא
4 יזוע ולא יתוב מן אנפי חרב [23]עלוהי יתלה שלט
5 שנן ונזך וחרף סיף ‹[24]›ולקל [25]קרנא יאמר האח ומן
6 רחיק יריח קרבה ולנקשת זין וזעקת אשתדור
7 יחדה [26]המן חכמתך יסתער נצא ויפרוס
8 כנפוה[י] לרוחין [27]או על מאמרך יתגב[ה] נש[רא
9 ועוזא ירים קנ[ה [28]ב]כפא ישכון ויקנן[
10 [29]]חפר אכל[א

Column XXXIV

(sixth column of the small scroll + fragm. N; Job xl 5-14 (15?))

1](5) [ ]סוף
2 [6]ענא אלהא לאיוב מן ר[וחא] ועננא ואמר לה אסר[7]
3 נא כגבר חלציך אשאלנך והתיבני פתגם [8]האף
4 תעדא דינה ותחיבנני על דברת די תזכא [9]או

4 For the meaning of *šlṭ* cf. Syriac *šelāṭā*, Brockelmann, pp. 780b/781a.

5 *nzk* « lance » is an Iranian loan-word, see W. W. Müller, Die Bedeutung des Wortes *'sprk* im Genesis-Apokryphon XXII, 31, *RQum* 2 (1959/60), pp. 445-447; J. C. Greenfield-S. Shaked, Three Iranian Words in the Targum of Job from Qumran, *ZDMG* 122 (1972), pp. 37-45, and cf.

gallops and rejoices, 3 and with force he sets out towards the sword. [22]He laughs at fear, he neither 4 trembles nor turns away from the sword. [23]He is hung about with 5 sharpened javelin, lance and whetted sword. [24/25]At the sound of the horn he says 'Aha!', from 6 afar he scents the battle and at the clashing of arms and the battle-cry 7 he rejoices.

[26]Is it by your wisdom that the falcon soars and spreads 8 its wings to the winds of heaven? [27]Or is it at your command that *the* eag*le* moun*t*s 9 and the black eagle makes *its* nest on high? [28]*On* the cliff it dwells and it builds its nest .... 10 .... [29]*From there* it spies out *the* prey ....

Column XXXIV
Job xl 5-14 (15?)

1 (5) ...... end.

2 [6]God answered Job from out of a w*ind* and a cloud and said to him: [7]Gird 3 up your loins like a man, then I will ask you, so give me an answer: [8]Would 4 you set aside the judgment and put me in the wrong

Syriac *nayzkā* « lance » (Brockelmann, p. 427b) and Arabic *nayzakun* « short lance ».
The targum is much shorter here than MT (verse 24).

XXXIV

1 *swp*: MT reads *ʾôsîp*.

2 *mn r*[*wḥʾ* is a supralinear addition correcting the textual error.

5 הא דרע כאלה איתי לך או בקל כותה תרעם
6 [10]העדי נא גוה ורם רוח וזוי והדר ויקר תלבש
7 [11]העדי נא חמת רגזך וחזא כל גאה והשפלה [12]וכל
8 רמת רוח תתבר והטפי רשיע[ין תחו]תיהון [13]וטמר
9 ית]הון בעפר כח]דא ק]טם תכסה
10] [14] (15?)]א איתי

Column XXXV

(seventh column of the small scroll; Job xl 23-31)

1 [[23]]
2 ירדנא גאפה יתרחץ די יקבלנה א..א
3 [24]במטל עינוהי יכלנה כבחכה יזיב אפה [25]התגד
4 תנין בחכא או בחבל תחרז לשנה [26]התשוא

5 *h'*: cf. Jastrow, s.v. (« is it that ? »).
Since "God" is written *'lh'* in the targum *'lh* obviously denotes a celestial being, cf. MT *'ēl*.

6/7 *h'dy* derives from *'d'* « to pass by » (cf. III, 7), in pael and haphel « to remove, set aside » (cf. line 4).

6 *zwy* must be equivalent to *zyw* « grandeur »; the form *zwy* is most probably a slip of the pen.

XXXV

2 *g'ph* probably derives from *gwp* « to (en)close » (pael with 3rd pers. sing. suffix referring to the equivalent of MT *b^e hēmôth*, Job xl 15).

that you may be in the right, [9]or 5 have you an arm like a celestial or can you thunder with a voice like his? 6 [10]Set aside haughtiness and pride, and put on grandeur and majesty and dignity! 7 [11]Set aside the heat of your anger, look upon all that is haughty and bring it down! [12]And all 8 that is proud—break it down, and blot out the wick*ed on* the *sp*ot; [13]hide 9 *th*em in the dust toge*ther*, cover *their* *faces with as*hes. 10 [14]....................... ....[(15?)].. there is

Column XXXV
Job xl 23-31

1 ....
.... [23]*if* 2 the Jordan encloses him, he trusts that ...... will receive him.
3 [24]Can one restrain him by covering his eyes, with perhaps a hook pierce his nose? [25]Can you draw 4
the crocodile with a hook, or pull a cord through his

MT *nāhār* has been replaced by *yrdn*ʾ from verse 23b.
yqblnh: the subject of the verb is uncertain but is probably to be found in the almost entirely damaged last word of the line (which seems to be a substantive, in view of the ending on *aleph*).

3 *mṭl* seems to be the infinitive of *ṭll* « to cover ». Covering the eyes is a means of taming an animal.
yzyb: the verb must mean « to pierce » or the like, but the root is not attested in the dictionaries.

3/4 *htgd tnyn*: here a new passage begins, dealing with *tnyn* « sea-monster, crocodile » (MT *liwyātān*).

5 זמם באפה ובחרתך תקוב לסתה [27]הימלל
6 עמך בניח או ימלל עמך בהתחננה לך [28]היקים
7 קים עמך ותדברנה לעבד עלם [29]התחאך
8 בה כצ[פרא ו]תקטרנה בחוטא לבנתך [30]וית[ ]ן
9 ע[לוהי]תין ויפלגון יתה בארע[ ]
10 [31]]נון די נונין[

Column XXXVI

(eighth column of the small scroll; Job xli 7-17)

1 [7]]]והי . .[[8]
2 לחדה ידבקן ורוח ל[א] תעול בינהן [9]אנתה
3 לחברתה חענן ולא יתפ[ר]שן [10]עטישתה תדלק
4 נורא בין עינוהי כממח פ[ר]א [11]מן פמה לפידין

5 *ḥrtk*: according to J. C. Greenfield-S. Shaked, Three Iranian Words in the Targum of Job from Qumran, *ZDMG* 122 (1972), pp. 37-45 *ḥrtk* is an Iranian loanword meaning « thorn ».

10 MT: *beṣilṣal dāgîm* « with a fish-hook »(?). Tg 2 reads *bgnwn' dnwny'* « in the shade (bridal chamber, breeding-place(?), cf. Jastrow s.v.) of fish », connecting *ṣilṣal* with the root *ṣll*. 11QtgJob may also have read *gnwn*, but palaeographically a word ending in *-nyn* or *-gwn* or *-gyn* is also possible. M. Sokoloff proposes to read *bdgwgyn* (*dy nwnyn*) « in fishing boats », cf. LXX: ἐν πλοίοις ἁλιέων.

XXXVI

2 The scales of the crocodile are the subject of the fem. plur. *ydbqn*.

tongue? [26]Can you put 5 a ring in his nose, and
pierce his jaw with a thorn? [27]Will he speak 6 with
you gently, or will he speak with you supplicatingly?
[28]Will he make 7 a covenant with you, and will
you take him as a slave for ever? [29]Will you play 8
with him like with a bi*rd*, *and* tie him with a string
for your daughters? [30]Will *trading-partne*rs 9 *haggle*
ov*er him*, and will they divide him in the land *of*
.... 10 [31]...............................
.... of fish ....

Column XXXVI
Job xli 7-17

1 [7]............................ his ....
.... [8]*One* 2 to another they stick together and
n*o* air comes between them. [9]Each 3 clasps its neighbour and they do not spring *a*part. [10]His sneezing
kindles 4 a fire between his eyes. As from a crate*r* (?)

3 *ḥʿnn*: part. plur. fem. of *ḥʿn*, probably cognate with Arabic *ḥḍn* and Accadian *ḫaṣanu* « to embrace ».

4 At the end of verse 10 MT has *keʿapʿappēy šāḥar* « as the eyelashes of dawn ». Apart from the fact that the *r* has been conjectured, it is not clear whether in our targum the corresponding Aramaic expression must be read as two separate words or one single word. In the first case the expression consists of the preposition *k* followed by the substantives *mmḥ* and *prʾ*, neither of which is known, unless *prʾ* must be connected with *šeparpārāʾ* « dawn » (Dan. vi 20), written in some oriental manuscripts as two separate words (*šepar pārāʾ*). In the second case the expression consists of *k* plus *min* plus the substantive *mḥprʾ* « mine », which might mean « crater » here.

5 יפקון בלשני אשה ירטון [12]מן נחירוה יפק תנן
6 לכוש יקד ומגמר [13]נפשה ג[מ]רין תגסא וזיקין
7 יפקן מן פמה [14]בצורה יבית תקפה וקדמוהי
8 תרוט עלימו [15]קפלי בשרה דבקין נסיכי[ן]
עלוהי
9 כפרזלא [16]ולבה[ ]ך כאבן[ ]ו[
10 [17]]..[ ]פח[דו]..[

Column XXXVII

(ninth column of the small scroll + fragm. R and J; Job xli 25-xlii 6)

1 [(25)]]...[ ]..ך[ ].[26] [
2 והוא מלך על כל רחש
3 [xlii 1]ענא איוב ואמר קדם אלהא [2]ידעת די כלא
4 תכול למעבד ולא יתבצר מנך תקף וחכמה
5 [xl 5]חדה מללת ולא אתיב ותרתין ועליהן לא

5 *yrṭwn*: cf. XXXIII, 2 (see also line 8 of our column). *nḥyrwh*: the *y* of the suffix seems to have been dropped accidentally, due to haplography.

6 *lkwš yqd wmgmr*: in this expression the preposition *l* either has the force of *k* or denotes a genitive construction. *mgmr* is attested in the Mishnah (Berakhoth VI, 6) as « burning spices ». Since Sperber in his edition of TJ reads *lkwš* in Zech. xii 6 instead of *lbwš*, which corresponds to MT *kiyyôr* « pot, basin », the possibility should not entirely be excluded that *lkwš* in our text renders MT *dûd* « pot ». In that case we have to translate « a burning and consuming pot ».

[11]from his mouth flames 5 come forth, like tongues of fire they flash. [12]From his nostrils comes forth smoke 6 as from reed on fire and burning spices. [13]His throat belches forth glowing co*a*ls; sparks 7 come forth from his mouth. [14]In his neck his strength is lodged, and ahead of him 8 power rushes along. [15]The folds of his flesh stick together, cas*t* on *him* 9 like iron. [16]*His* heart *is fir*m as a sto*ne* and ....
..... 10 [17].......... *are* afra*i*d ....

Column XXXVII
Job xli 25-xlii 6

1 (25) ....[26].....
.... 2 and he is king over all reptiles.
3 [xlii 1]Job began to speak and said to God: I know that 4 you can do all things, and that no strength or wisdom is beyond your power. 5 [xl 5]One thing I have spoken which I will not repeat; yea, two, to which no

gs' « to vomit » is attested here for the first time in Aramaic, but it is known from Syriac, see Brockelmann, p. 126b.

8 *qply bśrh*: since the verb *qpl* means « to fold » *qplyn* must denote the « folds » of the crocodile's body.

XXXVII

4 *ytbṣr mnk*: the expression has not been attested in Aramaic so far, but it is known from Syriac, cf. Gen. xi, 6 (Brockelmann, p. 86b « *effici non potuit* »).

5 The whole of line 5 and the first word of line 6 have no equivalent in MT Job xlii, but are taken over from ch. xl, 5, whereas MT xlii, 3 has been dropped here.

6 אוסף [xlii 4] שמע נא ואנה אמלל אשאלנך
7 והתיבני [5] למשמע אדן שמעתך וכען עיני
8 חזתך [6] על כן אתנסך ואתמהא ואהוא לעפר
9 וקטם] [ ]

COLUMN XXXVIII

(tenth column of the small scroll; Job xlii 9-11)

1].[ ]. .[ ][(9)]
2 אלהא ושמע אלהא בקלה די איוב ושבק
3 להון חטאיהון בדילה [10] ותב אלהא לאיוב
ברחמין
4 ויהב לה חד תרין בכל די הוא לה [11] ואתין לות
5 איוב כל רחמוהי וכל אחוהי וכל ידעוהי ואכלו
6 עמה לחם בביתה ונחמוהי על כל באישתה די
7 היתי אלהא עלוהי ויהבו לה גבר אמרה חדה
8 וגבר קדש חד די דהב

8 *ʾtnsk*: the targumist may have taken *ʾmʾs* as the 1st pers. imperf. niphal of *mʾs* II (« to be dissolved »), occurring in Ps. lviii 8 and Job vii 5. In the biblical text Job is depicted as repentant, because, in spite of the righteousness of his cause, he failed to recognize God's overpowering sovereignty, but in the targum Job remains the innocent sufferer. The terminology used here appears to be dependent on Ps. xxii, 15 f.

thing 6 I will add. [xlii] [4]Do listen, when I speak; when I ask you, 7 give me an answer. [5]By hearsay I have heard of you, but now my eye 8 has seen you.[6]Therefore I am poured out and I fall to pieces, and I become dust 9 and ashes. ....

Column XXXVIII
Job xlii 9-11

[9]*So Eliphaz the Temanite, Bildad the Shuhite,* 1 *and Zophar the Naamathite went and did as they were commanded by* 2 God; and God listened to the voice of Job and forgave 3 them their sins for his sake. [10]And God returned to Job in mercy 4 and gave him twice as much as all he had before. [11]Then came to 5 Job all his friends and all his brothers and all his acquaintances, and had 6 a meal with him in his house; and they consoled him for all the misfortune that 7 God had brought on him. And every one gave him a ewe-lamb 8 and every one a ring of gold.

XXXVIII

4 *ḥd tryn* « twice »: cf. B-L, § 95p.
ʾtyn: part. peal plur. of *ʾtʾ*. Cf. the last note on p. 89.

5 Job's sisters, mentioned in MT, are not referred to here, while MT « brothers » is substituted by « friends and brothers ».

8 *qdš* « ring ».

THE GENESIS APOCRYPHON FROM CAVE I
(1QGenAp)

INTRODUCTION

Together with six other scrolls the Genesis Apocryphon was discovered in cave 1 of Qumran in 1947. Like the so-called first Isaiah scroll (1QIs[a]), the Habakkuk commentary (1QpHab) and the Manual of Discipline (1QS) this writing came into the hands of the Syrian Metropolitan, Mar Athanasius Yeshue Samuel, the superior of St. Mark's monastery in the old city of Jerusalem. He had all these documents transferred to the U.S.A., but gave no permission for the badly preserved scroll of the Genesis Apocryphon to be opened and published, in spite of the fact that the other scrolls had already been published. A small fragment, broken off from the scroll, on which Lamech is referred to in the first person, gave rise to the idea that the scroll might be the lost apocryphal Book of Lamech, known only by name.

After the scrolls had come into the hands of the state of Israel, in 1954, work started immediately to open the severely damaged scroll with the help of the expertise of J. Biberkraut. It turned out that both the beginning and the end of the scroll were lost and that only small sections of many other columns were preserved. Part of column II and also columns XIX-XXII are in a fairly good state. The bad state of the rest of the scroll is not only due to a process of decay but also to the ink, which corroded the leather in many places.

Because of these difficulties only five columns

(II and XIX-XXII) were published in the *editio princeps* by N. AVIGAD-Y. YADIN, which the reader will find in the present edition, albeit with a number of corrections and additions to the official editors' transcription of the text. To their publication of the text AVIGAD and YADIN added an introduction in which they tried to tell what the other columns are about, going on the evidence from the little that is left.

When it was published, the document proved after all not to be the lost Book of Lamech, but a collection of haggadic traditions about Lamech, Henoch, Noah and Abraham. The narrative has a Biblical text as its basis, which is followed verse after verse so that one gets the impression now and then that it is a targum. Interwoven with the Biblical narratives we find stories which are the result of pious fantasy and a combination of texts based on Scripture study.

A striking feature is the attention paid to records of journeys and geographical details. As for its literary genre the work has its closest parallel in the Book of Jubilees, an Essene writing dating from the first century B.C.E., but it also corresponds with Eth. Henoch and other intertestamental writings. It is not impossible that the Genesis Apocryphon owes its existence to the religious community of Qumran.

The present manuscript can be dated to the latter half of the first century B.C.E. on palaeographical grounds, or to the beginning of the first half of the first century C.E. The philological evidence indicates that the writing itself dates from the first century B.C.E.

The language of 1QGenAp corresponds with the Aramaic of the book of Daniel, but represents a later stage (cf. e.g. the predominant use of *dy* (about 100x) instead of *d*[e] (8x); the use of *aleph* as preformative of the causative and reflexive conjugations of the verb; the predominance of the masculine demonstrative *dn* instead of the Biblical Aramaic *dnh*).

The contents of 1QGenAp can be summarized as follows:

Column I-V: The birth of Noah.

The portentous signs at Noah's birth cause Lamech to suspect that his wife Betenos had committed adultery with one of the divine beings (cf. Gen. vi 1-4). He goes to his father Methusalah, who refers him to Henoch, the beloved of the angels. In a long discourse Henoch sets his mind at ease.

Column VI-XVII: The life of Noah.

From VI, 6 onwards Noah is introduced in the first person. In this section of the scroll, which is severely damaged, it is told how Noah took a wife and how he took wives for his three sons, and the rest deals with the flood, the covenant God made with Noah, the planting of vines, and the allotment of land to Noah's sons.

Column XVIII-XXII: The Abram story.

After the description of Abram's journey from Ur of the Chaldees and Haran the author gives a detailed account of the journey to Egypt. The praises of Sarai's beauty, spoken by three Egyptian princes, came to the notice of the Pharaoh and Sarai was taken away from Abram and stayed for two years at the royal court. Afflicted by many plagues the Pharaoh was forced to restore her to Abram. After the group had left Egypt and settled in Bethel, Lot parted from his uncle. Thereafter God appeared to Abram in a vision of the night and commanded him to gaze from the hill of Ramath-Hazor in all directions and to look upon the whole of the promised land, and to walk through the whole of it. Following on this the journey of Chedorlaomer and the other kings is described, as well as Abram's encounter with Melchizedek and with the king of Sodom. The story breaks off at the end of column XXII where the author refers to the promise given to Abram that he will have a son.

LITERATURE

Text Publications:

N. Avigad-Y. Yadin, *A Genesis Apocryphon. A Scroll from the Wilderness of Judaea*, Jerusalem 1956 (*editio princeps*).

J. A. Fitzmyer, *The Genesis Apocryphon of Qumran Cave I. A Commentary* (Biblica et Orientalia 18A), Rome 1966, 1971².

Translations and Commentaries:

J. Carmignac- É. Cothenet-H. Lignée, *Les textes de Qumrân traduits et annotés* II, Paris 1963, pp. 205-242 (by Lignée).

J. A. Fitzmyer, see above.

J. Maier, *Die Texte vom Toten Meer*. I. Uebersetzung; II. Anmerkungen, München-Basel 1960 (I: pp. 157-165: translation; II: pp. 152-153: notes).

G. Vermes, *The Dead Sea Scrolls in English* (Pelican Book A 551), Harmondsworth 1962, pp. 216-224 (translation).

A. S. van der Woude, *Bijbelcommentaren en Bijbelse verhalen*, Amsterdam 1958, pp. 22-24; 95-112 (translation with concise notes).

Further Studies:

A full list of literature on 1QGenAp is provided by J. A. Fitzmyer, *o.c.*, 1971², pp. 41-45. Here we note the following studies:

H. Bardtke, Literaturbericht über Qumrān, Das Genesis-Apocryphon, *Theologische Rundschau* 37 (1972), pp. 193-219.

A. Dupont-Sommer, Exorcismes et guérisons dans les écrits de Qoumran, *Supplements to VT* VII (1960), pp. 246-261.

P. Grelot, Parwaïm des Chroniques à l'Apocryphe de la Genèse, *VT* 11 (1961), pp. 30-38.

P. Grelot, Sur l'Apocryphe de la Genèse (colonne XX, ligne 26), *RQum* 1 (1958/59), pp. 273-276.

P. Grelot, Retour au Parwaïm, *VT* 14 (1964), pp. 155-163.

E. Y. Kutscher, Dating the Language of the Genesis Apocryphon, *JBL* 76 (1957), pp. 288-292.

E. Y. Kutscher, The Language of the Genesis Apocryphon: A Preliminary Study, *Aspects of the Dead Sea Scrolls* (ScrHier 4), Jerusalem 1958, 1965², pp. 1-35.

M. R. Lehmann, 1Q Genesis Apocryphon in the Light of Targumim and Midrashim, *RQum* 1 (1958/59), pp. 249-263.

H. Lignée, Concordance de 1Q Genesis Apocryphon, *RQum* 1 (1958/59), pp. 163-186.

T. Muraoka, Notes on the Aramaic of the Genesis Apocryphon, *RQum* 8 (1972/....), pp. 7-51.

W. W. Müller, Die Bedeutung des Wortes *'sprk* im Genesis-Apokryphon XXII, 31, *RQum* 2 (1959/60), pp. 445-447.

E. Osswald, Beobachtungen zur Erzählung von Abrahams Aufenthalt in Ägypten im "Genesis-Apokryphon", *ZAW* 72 (1960), pp. 7-25.

H. H. Rowley, Notes on the Aramaic of the Genesis Apocryphon, *Hebrew and Semitic Studies Presented to G. R. Driver*, ed. by D. Winton Thomas and W. D. McHardy, Oxford 1963, pp. 116-129.

Col. II

(1) הא באדין חשבת בלבי די מן עירין הריאתא ומן
קדישין הריא ולנפיל[ין] (2) ולבי עלי משתני
על עולימא דנא (3) באדין אנה
למך אתבהלת ועלת על בתאנוש אנ[תתי ואמרת
] (4) אנה מועד בעליא במרה רבותא במלך
כול ע[למים] (5) [בני שמין עד כולא
בקושטא תחוינני הן] (6) [תחוינני

II

1 *ḥšbt*: the subject of the verb is Lamech, the father of Noah, cf. Gen. v 25 ff.

ʿyryn: a term signifying angels as astral powers, which occurs also in Dan. iv 10.14.20 and in pseudepigraphical writings, e.g. Jub., Eth. Hen., XII Patr.

qdyšyn: another term denoting angels, used in parallelism with *ʿîr(în)* in Dan. iv 10.14.20. It is a common term for angels in other Dead Sea Scrolls as well.

npylyn: the Aramaic equivalent of Hebrew *nephîlîm* signifying giants, who, according to Gen. vi 4, were on earth, when the "sons of God" had intercourse with the "daughters of men". In Jub. v 1 ff. and Eth. Hen. vii 2 it is explicitly said that these giants came from this intercourse. Here it must denote astral powers, cf. TJ Isaiah xiii 10.

hry'tʾ: in all likelihood the reading *hryʾntʾ* suggested by Kutscher and Fitzmyer (with a *nun*) « conception », must be abandoned, since the trace left on the manuscript, read as *nun*, seems to be due to a crack in the leather. In line 15 the form *hrywnʾ* « conception » occurs in the masculine, cf. *dn*.

Col. II

(1) Behold, then I thought to myself that she had conceived from the Watchers and had become pregnant by the Holy Ones, and that due to the Giant*s* ....., (2) and so my heart was troubled within me because of this child. (3) Then I, Lamech, made haste and went to *my* wif*e* Betenos *and I said*: "............ (4) I warn you solemnly by the Most High, by the Great Lord, by the King of all a*ges* .... (5) .... the Celestials, that you tell me everything truthfully, whether ..... (6) .... you must tell me without lies, whether

2 *ʿwlymʾ dnʾ*: *i.e.* Noah. For the signs and wonders in connection with his early childhood cf. Eth. Hen. cvi (fragment of the book of Noah).

3 *Betenos*: Lamech's cousin, known also from Jub. iv 28.

4 *ʾnh mwʿd*: the reading *ʾnʾ wʿd* of the *editio princeps* cannot be substantiated with evidence from the manuscript; *mwʿd* is the aphel participle of *yʿd* « forewarn », cf. Jastrow *s.v.*
ʿlyʾ: an epithet of God, occurring in Dan. iii 26.32; iv 14; v 18.21, and frequently in intertestamental literature. Cf. also 4QOrNab I, 2.
mrh rbwtʾ: cf. Eth. Hen. lxxxi 3.
mlk kwl ʿlmym: cf. II, 7; XX, 13; XXI, 10.12, and Jub. xxxi 13; see also 1 Tim. i 17.

5 *bny šmyn*: in later Jewish literature the term *šmyn* is often a substitute for "God". Therefore this expression is the equivalent of Hebr. *bᵉnēy ʾᵉlōhîm* « divine beings ».
ʿd: there is enough evidence to show that *ʿd* is an abbreviated form of *ʿd dy/zy* « so that », cf. Driver xi, 3 with Cowley 30, 27; 31, 26.

ולא בכדבין הדא ב[ ] (7) במלך
כול עלמים עד בקושט עמי תמללין ולא בכדבין [
] (8) אדין בתאנוש אנתתי בחלץ תקיף
עמי מללת וב[ ] (9) ואמרת יא אחי
ויא מרי דכרלך על עדינתי א[ ]
(10) בחום ענתא ונשמתי לגו נדנהא ואנה בקושט
כול[א (11)]ול.. שגי
לבי עלי אדין אשתני (12) וכדי חזת
בתאנוש אנתתי די אשתני אנפי עלי ..[
] (13) באדין אנסת רוחהא ועמי תמלל ולי תאמר
יא מרי ויא אחי [דכרלך] (14) עדינתי יאמיא אנה
לך בקדישא רבא במלך ש[מיא]
(15) די מנך זרעא דן ומנך הריונא דן ומנך נצבת
פריא[ ] (16) ולא מן כול זר ולא מן כול
עירין ולא מן כול בני שמ[ין] (17) אנפיך
כדנא עליך שנא ושחת ורוחך כדן עליבא[
] (18) בקושט ממללא עמך
(19) באדין אנה למך רטת על מתושלח אבי וכולא

7 *ʿd*: cf. line 5.

9 *yʾ ʾḥy*: a solemn form of address.
ʿdynty: cf. Hebrew *ʿèdnāh* « sexual pleasure », Gen. xviii 12 (cf. also Is. xlvii 8).

10 *nšmty lgw ndnhʾ*: for this metaphor cf. Dan. vii 15. The third sing. fem. suff. *-hʾ* is quite common in 1QGenAp.

11 Since *ʾdyn* always seems to introduce a new phrase the words preceding it should be taken separately, which

this .... (7) by the King of all ages, that you speak to me truthfully, without lies ...." (8) Then my wife Betenos spoke to me with great vehemence and .... (9) and she said: "O my brother and my lord, remember my sexual pleasure .... (10) in the excitement of intercourse, and my panting breath in the midst of its body. I truthfully all ...." (11) .... very much my heart within me, it was still troubled. (12) And when my wife Betenos saw that my countenance was troubled .... (13) then she suppressed her emotion, talked with me and said to me: "O my lord and my brother, *remember* (14) my sexual pleasure. I swear to you by the great Holy One, by the King of he*aven* .... (15) that from you is this seed, from you is this pregnancy and from you *this* fruit planted .... (16) and not from any stranger, not from any of the Watchers and not from any of the Celesti*als* .... *Let not* (17) your countenance be so troubled and upset and your spirit be so depressed ..... (18) I am speaking to you truthfully". (19) Then

means that the current translation: "and then my mind was much changed within me" is very unlikely. In view of line 2 *ʾdyn* can here only mean «still». The reading of the word preceding *śgy* (probably a verb) remains problematic.

14 *yʾmyʾ*: sing. fem. participle of *ymʾ* « to swear ».

19 For Methuselah, the father of Lamech, cf.Gen. v 21 ff. The restoration of the end of the line is based on Eth. Hen. cvi 7 (fragment of the Book of Noah).

לה חו[ית חנוך] (20) אבוהי וכולא מנה

ביצבא ינדע בדי הוא רחים ורעי[אלהא ועם

קדישיא] (21) עדבה פליג ולה מחוין כולא

וכדי שמע מתושל[ח] (22) רט לחנוך

אבוהי למנדע מנה כולא בקושטא[ ]

(23) רעותה ואזל לארך מת לפרוין ותמן אשכחה

לחנוך [אבוהי] (24) ו]אמר לחנוך אבוהי

יא אבי ויא מרי די אנה לך ··[(25)]ל[

]ואמר לך דאל תרגז עלי די להכא אתית ל····[

(26)]·ל לעליך(?)[

(27) ·ל[

COL. XIX

(7) ובנית תמן מדבח]א

[וקרית] תמ[ן בשם א]ל[הא] ואמרת אנתה הוא (8)

20 *'bwhy*: *i.e.* Henoch, cf. Gen. v 18 ff., the great sage of primeval times who was considered to know all mysteries, because the angels of God showed him "everything which is on earth and in the heavens" (Jub. iv 21; Eth. Hen. i 2).

At the end of the line we propose to read *r'y* (peîl) « favourite », cf. Hebr. xi 5.

23 *l'rk mt*: though neither the reading nor the meaning of these words can be ascertained, we follow the interpretation of FITZMYER.

prwyn: cf. 2 Chron. iii 6, the name of a mythological region, considered to be the paradise of the righteous

I, Lamech, sped to my father Methuselah and to*ld* him everything. *I asked him to go to Henoch* (20) his father, that he might learn everything from him with certainty, since he is the beloved and the favouri*te of God and with the Holy Ones* (21) his lot is apportioned, and to him they make everything known. And when Methusela*h* heard .... (22) he sped to his father Henoch in order to learn from him everything truthfully .... (23) his will. And he went through the length of the land to Parvaim and there he found Hen*och, his father* .... (24) *and* he said to his father Henoch: "O my father and my lord, to whom I .... (25) .... I beg you, do not be angry with me for having come here in order to ...... (26) ....
....
.... (27) ....

Col. XIX

(7) .... *and I built there an altar, I called* ther*e upon the name of G*od and I said: "You are (8) *my God,*

(cf. P. Grelot, VT 11 (1961), pp. 30-38; 14 (1964), pp. 155-163).

26 What is left of this line cannot be restored with any certainty.

XIX

The numbering of the lines in the *editio princeps* is not correct, line 7 being the 6th and so on. In order, however, to avoid confusion we follow the numbering of the *editio princeps*.

7-8 The restoration of these lines is based on col. XXI, 1 f., Gen. xii 8 and Jub. xiii 8.

א]ל[הי א]ל[ה ע]ל[מיא ותמן ה]לל[ת וברכת מרה
כו]ל עלמים עד כען לא דבקתה לטורא קדישא
ונגדת (9) ל[מוריה] והוית אזל לדרומא [ ]א..
עד די דבקת לחברון ל[ ]אתב[נ]יאת חברון
ויתבת (10) [תמן תרת]ין [שנין] והוא
כפנא בארעא דא כולא ושמעת די ע[בו]רא ה[וא]
במצרין ונגדת (11) ל[מעל] לארע מצרין [ ]א
די .ל[עד די דבק]ת לכרמונא
נהרא חד מן (12) ראשי נהרא ..ל[ ]ל[ ]
כען אנחנא [ ] ארענא [וח]לפת שבעת ראשי
נהרא דן די (13) ..[ ]לל[ ]מל[ ]א
כען חלפנא ארענא ועלנא לארע בני חם לארע מצרין
(14) וחלמת אנה אברם חלם בלילה
מעלי לארע מצרין וחזית בחלמי [וה]א ארז חד
ותמרא (15) חדא ...א...[ ]וב[ני] אנוש אתו
ובעין למקץ ולמעקר ל[א]רזא ולמשבוק תמרתא

ṭwrʾ qdyšʾ: almost certainly the mountain on which Solomon's temple was built.

ngdt: the starting-point of Abram's journey is Bethel, cf. Gen. xii 8.

9 *Moriah*: For this conjecture cf. Gen. xxii 2, *ṭwrʾ qdyšʾ* in line 8 and *ṭwr mwryh* in Neofiti 1, Gen. xxii 2.
For the tradition that Hebron was built seven years before Zoan-Tanis cf. Numb. xiii 22; Jub. xiii 10.12.

10 *two years*: cf. Jub. xiii 10.

11 *ʿd dy dbqt*: cf. line 9; the reading *whwʾ dbqt*, proposed in the *editio princeps*, also accepted by FITZMYER, is grammatically impossible.

God eternal". *And there I praised and blessed the Lord of a*ll ages. Up till then I had not reached the holy mountain; so I set out (9) for *Moriah* and I kept going southward .... until I reached Hebron; at *that time* Hebron was b*ui*lt, and I dwelt (10) *there for tw*o *years*. And there was a famine all over that country, but I heard that *there* w*as* gr*ai*n in Egypt; so I set out (11) in order to *enter* the land of Egypt .... which .... *until* I *reached* the Carmon River, one of the (12) streams of the River .... At that moment we *left* our land, and I *cro*ssed the seven streams of this river, which (13) ....; so we left our land and entered the land of the sons of Ham, the land of Egypt. (14)
I, Abram, had a dream in the night of my entering into the land of Egypt, and I saw in my dream *there w*as a cedar, and a palm- (15) tree ....; and peo*p*le came intending to cut down and uproot

krmwn' nhr': this river should in all probability be identified with the *Qeramiyôn*, mentioned in Mishnah Parah viii, 8 and bab. Baba Bathra 74b, one of the four rivers surrounding the land of Israel.

12 *nhr'*: *i.e.* the Nile.

15 *b'yn*: part. masc. plur. of *b''*. The reading *b'wn* (*editio princeps*), supposed to be the 3rd pers. plur. of the perfect, can hardly be expected in an Aramaic text as early as this one, cf. the preceding verbal form *'tw* (without a *nun!*).

בלחודיהה (16) ואכליאת תמרתא ואמרת אל תקוצו
ל[א]רזא ארי תרינא מן שר.[ ]א ושביק ארזא בטלל
תמרתא (17) ולא [אתקץ] ואתעירת
בליליא מן שנתי ואמרת לשרי אנתתי חלם (18) חלמת
[אנה וא]דחל [מן] חלמא דן ואמרת לי אשתעי לי
חלמך ואנדע ושרית לאשתעיא לה חלמא דן (19)
[וחוית] ל[ה פשר] חלמא [דן]די
יבעון למקטלני ולכי למשבק [ב]רם דא כול טבותא
(20) [די תעבדין עמי] בכול [אתר] די [נהוה בה אמרי]
עלי די אחי הוא ואחי בטליכי ותפלט נפשי בדליכי
(21) [יבעון] לאע[ד]יותכי מני
ולמקטלני ובכת שרי על מלי בליליא דן (22) [
]ל .ל[ ]. ופרעו צ[ען]ל[

16 *tryn*ʾ: reading to be preferred to *tryp*ʾ (*editio princeps*); H. L. Ginsberg's conjecture (*mn*) *šrb*ʾ *ḥd*ʾ « from one family », accepted by Fitzmyer, is much to short in view of the space available.

18 Since the space available requires another word before *wʾdḥl* we propose to read *ʾnh*, cf. line 14.

19 *brm*: obviously synonymous with *blḥwd* in line 15 as shown by the parallel phrasing; for the adverbial use of *brm* meaning « only » compare TO Gen. vii 23 (*brm*) with Neofiti 1, Gen. vii 23 (*lḥwd*).

the *ce*dar but to leave the palm-tree by itself. (16) But the palm-tree cried out and said: "Do not cut down the *ce*dar, for both of us are from ...."; so the cedar was spared by the protection of the palm-tree (17) and *was* not *cut down.*
During the night I awoke from my sleep and I said to my wife Sarai: "I have had (18) a dream *and I* am frightened *because of* that dream". She said to me: "Tell me your dream that I may know it". So I began to tell her that dream (19) *and I made known* to *her the meaning of that* dream ....
".... who intend to kill me and to spare you *on*ly. This is the only favour (20) *that you must do for me*: at every *place wh*ere *we shall be, say* about me: 'he is my brother'; then I shall stay alive by your protection and my life shall be saved because of you. (21)
....
... *they will try* to ta*k*e you away from me and to kill me". Then Sarai wept over my words that night (22) ....
.... and Pharaoh Zo*an* ....

20 For the restoration of the first part of this line cf. TO and Neofiti I, Gen. xx 13.
bṭlyky: the word *ṭl* is a parallel form of *ṭll* « shade, protection », cf. line 16; both forms are attested in *Reichsaramäisch*, see COWLEY 38, 5; Behistun 5.13. For the rather unusual suffix form (cf. also *bdlyky* at the end of the line) cf. *zylyky*, COWLEY 8, 19.

21 *lʾʿdywtky*: inf. constr. aphel of *ʿdʾ* with *l* and the suffix of the 2nd pers. sing. fem.

22 *prʿw ṣʿn*: the pharaoh is named after his residential city.

] ל... שרי למפנה לצען (23) [עמי והסתמרת
י]תירא בנפשה די לא יחזנה כול [אנש חמש שני]ן
ולבתר חמש שניא אלן (24) [אתו] תלתת גברין מן
רברבי מצרי]ן] די פרע[ו] צע[ן] על
מל[י] ועל אנתתי והווא יהבין (25) [לי מתנן שגיאן
ובעו] ל[י] ל[אודעא] טבתא וחכמתא וקושטא וקרית
קודמיהון ל[כתב] מלי חנוך (26) [ ]
כפנא(?) די[ ]א... ולא[ ]ין למקם עד די
....ם ל..[ ]מלי (27) [ ]ל[
]במאכל שגי ובמשתה[
]חמרא (28) [

Col. XX

(1) ...[ ]א..[ ]..[ ]....[
(2)].ל..]...[
לה ושפיר .צ.. כמה ....
צלם אנפיהא וכמא (3) [נ]עים ומא רקיק לה שער
ראישה כמא יאין להון לה עיניהא ומא רגג הוא לה
אנפהא וכול נץ (4) אנפיהא ... כמא יאא לה חדיה

23 For the five years cf. Jub. xiii 11.

25 The triad *ṭbtʾ wḥkmtʾ wqwšṭʾ* can best be interpreted as expressing one idea; the noun connoting the main idea is qualified by the other two.

.... Sarai *re-frained* from going to Zoan (23) *with me*; *and she was very* much on her *guard* that no*body* would see her, *five year*s long. But after those five years (24) *there came* three men from among the princes of Egyp*t* .... of Phar*aoh* Zoa*n* because of *my* words and because of my wife, and they gave (25) *me many gifts and asked* me to *make known* good and true wisdom. Then I recited to them the *Book* of the words of Henoch (26) .... the famine (?) which .... and not .... *and* they *decided* to stay until .... the words of (27) .... with much eating and drinking .... the wine

Col. XX

(1)
(2) "........................ *how* ....
... and beautiful is the form of her face and how (3) *lo*vely and how fine is the hair of her head; how graceful in it are her eyes and what a desirable thing is her nose and all the blossom of (4) her face is ....; how graceful is her breast and how beautiful

XX

3 *lhwn*: we take the *l* of this form as a possessive *lamed* referring to *ʾnpyhʾ* and *rʾyšh*.
rgg: obviously a substantive in the absolute state.

4 *lbnhʾ*: in ancient times a fair skin was considered to be a sign of beauty.

וכמא שפיר לה כול לבנהא דרעיהא מא שפירן
וידיהא כמא (5) כלילן ומא . .ל מחזה יד[י]הא כמא
יאין כפיהא ומא אריכן וקטינן כול אצבעת ידיהא
רגליהא (6) כמא שפירן וכמא שלמא להן לה שקיהא
וכל בתולן וכלאן די יעלן לגנון לא ישפרן מנהא ועל
כול (7) נשין שופר שפרה ועליא שפרהא לעלא מן
כולהן ועם כול שפרא דן חכמא שגיא עמהא
ודלידיהא (8) יאא וכדי שמע מלכא מלי חרקנוש ומלי
תרין חברוהי די פם חד תלתהון ממללין שגי רחמה
ושלח (9) לעובע דברהא וחזהא ואתמה על כול
שפרהא ונסבהא לה לאנתא ובעא למקטלני ואמרת
שרי (10) למלכא דאחי הוא כדי הוית מתגר על
דילהא ושביקת אנה אברם בדילהא ולא קטילת

5 *wm'*: the most possible reading in view of the traces of letters, and in view of the fact that the same phrasing (*km'*. . . . .*wm'*) occurs in line 3 and further on in line 5. The following word, obviously an adjective, cannot be reconstructed with any certainty except for the final *l*.

6 *šlm'*: obviously a substantive, cf. l.3; *lhn* refers to *rglyh'* (feminine!), cf. the note on *lhwn* in line 3.
kl'n: absolute state plural of *klt'*, usually written *kln*.

7 *šwpr šprh*: a *figura etymologica* in which the noun *šwpr* intensifies the verbal form (feminine participle) *šprh*.
'ly': feminine participle of *'l'* « to go up, to rise »; for the final *aleph* cf. *y'my'* in II, 14.

is her white colour; her arms, how beautiful they are! Her hands, how (5) perfect they are and how .... is the appearance of her hands! How graceful are her palms, and how slender and fine are all the fingers of her hands; her legs, (6) how beautiful they are, and what perfect things thereof are her thighs! There are no virgins or brides, who enter the bridal canopy, more beautiful than she, and above all (7) women she excels in beauty and her beauty surpasses all of them. In addition to all this beauty there is much wisdom in her, yea what is hers (8) is graceful." When the king heard the words of Horqanosh and the words of his two companions, all three of whom spoke as with one mouth, he passionately fell in love with her, and (9) at once ordered that she be brought. And when he saw her, he marvelled at all her beauty and took her to him to be his wife. Then he sought to kill me, but Sarai said (10) to the king: "He is my brother", whereupon I was benefited because of her. So I, Abram, was spared thanks to her and I was not

*dlydyh*ʾ: a compound word made up of the elements *d* (= *dy*) + *l* + *yad* (dual) + suffix fem. sing.

8 *ḥrqnwš*: an Egyptian personal name, cf. P. Grelot, Un nom égyptien dans l'Apocryphe de la Genèse, *RQum* VII, 1969-1971, pp. 557-566.

pm ḥd: cf. Hebr. *pèh* ʾ*èḥād* in Josh. ix 2 and 1 Ki. xxii 13.

9 *l*ʿ*wb*ʿ: cf. the note on 11QtgJob III, 7.

10 *mtgr*: most scholars rightly derive this form from the verb *tgr* which in the ithpe. and ithpa. means « to make profit, to be benefited », cf. also MT Gen. xii 16.

ובכית אנה (11) אברם בכי תקיף אנה ולוט בר אחי
עמי בליליא כדי דבירת מני שרי באונס
(12) בליליא דן צלית ובעית ואתחננת ואמרת
באתעצבא ודמעי נחתן בריך אנתה אל עליון מרי
לכול (13) עלמים די אנתה מרה ושליט על כולא
ובכול מלכי ארעא אנתה שליט למעבד בכולהון
דין וכען (14) קבלתך מרי על פרעו צען מלך מצרין
די דברת אנתתי מני בתוקף עבד לי דין מנה ואחזי
ידך רבתא (15) בה ובכול ביתה ואל ישלט בליליא
דן לטמיא אנתתי מני וינדעוך מרי די אנתה מרה לכול
מלכי (16) ארעא ובכית וחשית בליליא דן שלח לה
אל עליון רוח מכדש למכתשה ולכול אנש ביתה רוח

12/13 *mry lkwl ʿlmym*: cf. II, 4.7; XXI, 10.12.

14 *qbltk*: for *qbl* used either with *qdm* (« before ») or with an accusative in a juridical sense, cf. Cowley 6,5; 8,13; 10,12; 47,7. See also J. A. Fitzmyer, *JNES* 21, 1962, p. 19.

dbrt: peîl form.

mnh: the preposition *mn* is used here to express contradistinction, cf. MT Gen. xxxviii 26; 1 Sam. xxiv 18; 1 Ki ii 32, and παρά in Luke xviii 14.

ʾḥzy: imperative aphel.

15 *lṭmyʾ*: cf. MT Lev. xviii 20; Ez. xviii 6.11.15; xxii 11; xxxiii 26.

killed. And I wept, I, (11) Abram, with bitter weeping, I and Lot my brother's son with me, that night when Sarai was taken away from me by force. (12) That night I prayed, I begged and implored, and I said in (my) grief, while my tears ran down: "Blessed art Thou, God Most High, my Lord, for all (13) ages, Thou who art Lord and Ruler over all, yea among all the kings of the earth Thou art the One who has the power to execute judgment among them all, and now (14) I cry out to Thee, my Lord, against Pharaoh Zoan, the king of Egypt, because my wife has been taken away from me by force. Put me in the right, not him, and show forth Thy mighty hand (15) against him and against all his house, and do not let him tonight be able to make my wife unclean to me, so that it may be known about Thee, my Lord, that Thou art Lord of all the kings of (16) the earth." Thus I wept and suffered. That night God Most High sent to him a pestilent spirit to afflict

mny: here the preposition *mn* has a separative force (« away from me »). Sarai's defilement would make her legally no longer acceptable to Abram.

16 *ḥšyt*: this form most probably comes from *ḥšʾ* (= *ḥwš* = *ḥšš*) « to suffer », to be distinguished from *ḥšʾ* « to be silent ».

mkdš: probably a substantive, rather than a participle aphel, an alternate form of *mktš* owing to partial dissimilation. For *mktš* denoting the plagues of Egypt cf. TO Deut. xxviii 60, and cf. the targums on Gen. xii 17.

rwḥ bʾyšʾ: an apposition to *rwḥ mkdš*. For the term cf. Luke vii 21; Acts xix 12.13.15.16; Eth. Hen. xv 8 ff.

(17) באישא והואת כתשא לה ולכול אנש ביתה ולא
יכל למקרב בהא ואף לא ידעהא והוא עמה (18)
תרתין שנין ולסוף תרתין שנין תקפו וגברו עלוהי
מכתשיא ונגדיא ועל כול אנש ביתה ושלח (19) קרא
לכול חכימ[י] מצרין ולכול אשפיא עם כול אסי
מצרין הן יכולון לאסיותה מן מכתשא דן ולאנש (20)
ביתה ולא יכלו כול אסיא ואשפיא וכול חכימיא
למקם לאסיותה ארי הוא רוחא כתש לכולהון (21)
וערקו באדין אתה עלי
חרקנוש ובעא מני די אתה ואצלה על (22) מלכא
ואסמוך ידי עלוהי ויחה ארי ב[ח]לם חז[ני] ואמר לה
לוט לא יכול אברם דדי לצליא על (23) מלכא ושרי
אנתתה עמה וכען אזל אמר למלכא וישלח אנתתה
מנה לבעלהא ויצלה עלוהו ויחה (24)
וכדי שמע חרקנוש מלי לוט אזל אמר למלכא כול

17 *whw'*: for palaeographical reasons this reading is to be preferred to *why'*.

18 *trtyn šnyn*: the same period is presupposed in Jub. xiii 11 ff.

20 *lmqm l'sywth*: literally « to rise to heal him », *'sywth* being most probably the inf. constr. pael of *'s'*, with suffix.

21 *'th*: 1st person singular imperf. peal of *'t'* with elision of the first root letter.

him, and to all the men of his house—an evil (17) spirit, and it kept afflicting him and all the men of his house, so he was not able to approach her nor did he have intercourse with her though he was in her company (18) for two years. At the end of two years the afflictions and the punishments became severe and harsh on him and on all the men of his house. So he sent (19) for all the sages of Egypt and all the magicians, together with all the physicians of Egypt, to see if they could heal him from that affliction, as well as the men of (20) his house. But none of the physicians and magicians, nor any of the sages could bring about his healing, for the spirit afflicted them all (21) and they fled. Thereupon Horqanosh came to me and begged me to come and to pray for (22) the king and to lay my hands upon him that he might recover, because he had seen *me* in a *dr*eam. But Lot said to him: "My uncle Abram cannot pray for (23) the king while his wife Sarai is with him. Therefore, go and tell the king to send that wife away from him, back to her husband. Then he will pray for him that he may recover". (24)

Now when Horqanosh heard Lot's words he

22 *ʾsmwk*: the practice of the laying on of hands as an act of exorcism is well attested in the New Testament, cf. especially Mark v 23 where the verb ζάω has the same connotation as *ḥyʾ* in our text (cf. also MT 2 Ki. viii 8.10). *yḥh*: short form of the 3rd pers. masc. sing. imperf. peal of *ḥyʾ*.

23 (*wyšlḥ*) *ʾntth*: literally « his wife » i.e. Abram's wife.

מכתשיא ונגדיא (25) אלן די מתכתש ומתנגד מרי
מלכא בדיל שרי אנתת אברם יתיבו נה לשרי לאברם
בעלה (26) ויתוך מנכה מכתשא דן ורוח שחלניא וקרא
לי [מ]ל[כא] ואמר לי מא עבדתה לי בדיל [שר]י
ותאמר (27) לי די אחתי היא והיא הואת אנתתך
ונסבתהא לי לאנתה הא אנתתך דברה אזל ועדי לך
מן (28) כול מדינת מצרין וכען צלי עלי ועל ביתי
ותתגער מננה רוחא דא באישתא וצלית על [די
ית]רפא (29) הו וסמכת ידי על [ראי]שה ואתפלי מנה
מכתשא ואתגערת [מנה רוחא] באישתא וחי וקם ויהב
(30) לי מלכא ב[יומא ד]נא מנתנ[ן] שגיאן וימא לי
מלכא במומה די לא . . .הא ו[   ]הא ואתיב לי
(31) לשרי ויהב לה מלכא [כסף וד]הב [ש]גיא ולבוש

26 *ytwk*: this form derives from the root *twk*, cf. Syr. *tk* « to desist from ».
*šḥlny*ʾ: not *šḥlnp*ʾ as printed in the *editio princeps*. The substantive derives from the root *šḥl* (Syr. « to flow »), and is related to Syr. *šāḥlānāyā*ʾ (adj.) « running, putrid, pussy », cf. P. Grelot, *RQum* 1 (1958-1959), pp. 273-276.
*mlk*ʾ: since the reading ʾ*lw* proposed by the *editio princeps* is untenable (Hebrew!), we suggest to read *mlk*ʾ, which supplies the new subject required in the context.

28 *ʿl dy ytrp*ʾ: the second last letter of the line is clearly a

went and said to the king: "All these afflictions and punishments (25) with which my lord the king is afflicted and punished are because of Sarai, the wife of Abram. So let Sarai be brought back to Abram her husband, (26) and this affliction will depart from you, the spirit of purulence". Then the ki*ng* summoned me and said to me: "What have you done to me because of *Sar*ai, that you told (27) me: 'She is my sister', while she was your wife, so that I took her to be my wife? Here is your wife! take her away, leave and depart from (28) the whole territory of Egypt. But now pray for me and for my house that this evil spirit be expelled from us". So I prayed *that* he *be* cured, (29) and I laid my hands upon his *hea*d and the plague was removed from him and *the* evil *spirit* was expelled *from him* and he recovered. Then the king rose and gave (30) me on *tha*t *day* many gif*ts* and the king swore me with an oath that he had not .... her and .... her. And he brought back to me (31) Sarai. Then the king gave her *m*uch *silver and g*old, much clothing of fine linen and purple and ....

pe, not a *nun* as printed in the *editio princeps*, whereas the preceding letter is rather a *reš* than a *dalet*; the verb *rp*ʾ « to heal » is attested in Hebrew (cf. Gen. xx 17) and in Syriac.

29 *qm wyhb*: the reading *qm hwd*ʿ as proposed in the *editio princeps* is most improbable, since the context requires a verb expressing a gesture of gratitude on the part of the king. Our reading *wyhb* is fully justified on palaeographical grounds.

30 *w*ʾ*tyb ly lśry*: cf. line 25.

שגי די בוץ וארגואן ו[ ] (32) קודמיהא
ואף להגר וא[ש]למה לי ומני עמי אנוש די ינפק[ונני
] (33) ואזלת אנה אברם בנכסין
שגיאין לחדא ואף בכסף ודהב וסלקת מן [מצרי]ן
[ואזל לוט] (34) בר אחי עמי ואף לוט קנה לה נכסין
שגיאין ונסב לה אנתה מן בנת [מצרין] והוית ש[רא

Col. XXI

(1) בכל אתר משריאתי עד די דבקת לבית אל
לאתרא די בנית תמן בה מדבחא ובניתה תניאני (2)
[ו]אקרבת עלוהי עלואן ומנחה לאל עליון וקרית
תמן בשם מרה עלמיא והללת לשם אלהא וברכת
(3) [א]להא ואודית תמן קודם אלהא על כול נכסיא
וטבתא די יהב לי ודי עבד עמי טב ודי אתיבני (4)
לארעא דא בשלם
(5) בתר יומא דן פרש לוט מן לואתי מן עובד רעותנא

32 *hgr*: since Gen. xvi 1 refers to Hagar as an Egyptian handmaid it is most natural that in later tradition she was thought to have been given to Sarai by the pharaoh.

33 *'nth mn bnt mṣryn*: the provenance of Lot's wife is mentioned neither in the Old Testament nor in the book of Jubilees.

XXI

1 *tny'ny*: this form, probably influenced by post-exilic

(32) before her, and also Hagar. He h*and*ed her (Sarai) over to me and appointed for me men who would escort *me* ... out *of Egypt.* (33)
So I, Abram, went with very many flocks and also with silver and gold, and I went up from *Egyp*t. *And Lot,* (34) my brother's son, *went* with me. Lot too had acquired many flocks and had taken for himself a wife from the daughters *of Egypt.* I ca*mp*ed

Col. XXI

(1) at every place of my encampments, until I reached Bethel, the place where I had built an altar, and I built it again, (2) *and* I offered upon it burnt offerings and a meal offering to God Most High and I called there upon the name of the Lord of ages and I praised the name of God and I blessed (3) God. So there I gave thanks to God for all the herds and the good things which He had given me, because He had done good to me and because He had brought me back (4) to this land in safety.
(5) After this day Lot parted from me because of the conduct of our herdsmen; he went to settle in the

Hebrew, cf. *šēnî* « again » Neh. iii, 30, is attested in Samaritan Aramaic (cf. Kutscher, p. 13), where the word is also used adverbially: « for the second time, again ». It corresponds to Biblical Aramaic *tinyānût* (Dan. ii 7) and Samaritan Aramaic *tinyānû*.

3 *qwdm*: this preposition is often used in the targums instead of the accusative or *l*, to stress God's transcendence.

ואזל ויתב לה בבקעת ירדנא וכול נכסוהי (6) עמה
ואף אנה אוספת לה על דילה שגי והוא רעה נכסוהי
ודבק עד סודם וזבן לה בסודם בי (7) ויתב בה ואנה
הוית יתב בטורא די בית אל ובאש עלי די פרש לוט
בר אחי מן לואתי (8) ואתחזי
לי אלהא בחזוא די ליליא ואמר לי סלק לך לרמת
חצור די על שמאל (9) ביתאל אתר די אנתה יתב
ושקול עיניך וחזי למדנחא ולמערבא ולדרומא
ולצפונא וחזי כול (10) ארעא דא די אנה יהב לך
ולזרעך לכול עלמים וסלקת למחרתי כן לרמת
חצור וחזית ארעא מן (11) רמתא דא מן נהר מצרין
עד לבנן ושניר ומן ימא רבא עד חורן וכול ארע גבל

6 *whwʾ*: verbal form.
wzbn: the reading *wybn* found in the *editio princeps* must be excluded, since the imperf. cons. does not occur in Aramaic.
by: alternate form of *bayit* « house », as an absolute state not uncommon in Official Aramaic (Cowley 3, 18; 8, 35; 9, 3; 10, 9; 82, 8; Aḥiqar, 125), but also found as early as the 8th century B.C.E. (Bar-Rekub inscription, line 16).

7 *wbʾš ʿly*: cf. Dan. vi 15.

8 *rmt ḥzwr*: this height is situated about 5 miles northeast of Bethel, rising 3300 feet above sea level (modern *jebel el-ʿAṣur*). It is to be identified with Baal Hazor in 2 Sam. xiii 23.

10 *lmḥrty kn*: in this phrase *mḥrty* has the force of a preposition and has obviously been formed on the analogy of *ʾaḥ^a^rēy* in the phrase *ʾaḥ^a^rēy kēn* « after this, thereafter ».

valley of the Jordan, together with all his herds, (6) and I also added much to what he had. Pasturing his herds he reached Sodom and he bought himself a house in Sodom (7) and settled in it. But I remained in the hill country of Bethel, and it grieved me that my nephew Lot had parted from me. (8)
Then God appeared to me in a vision of the night and said to me: "Go up to Ramath-Hazor which is north of (9) Bethel, the place where you live, and lift up your eyes and look to the east, the west, the south and the north, and behold all (10) this land which I give to you and to your progeny for ever". So the next day I went up to Ramath-Hazor and I beheld the land from (11) that height, from the River of Egypt to Lebanon and Senir, and from the Great Sea to Hauran, and all the land of Gebal as far as

11 *nhr mṣryn*: this name denotes the Gihon, cf. line 15, and must be identified with the Nile, cf. Gen. xv 18 which must also refer to the Nile and not to the "Brook of Egypt" (*Wadi el-ʿArîš*), elsewhere mentioned as the southern border of Canaan e.g. Num. xxxiv 5 and Is. xxvii 12.

śnyr: the Anti-Lebanon; according to Deut. iii 9 Senir was the Amorite name for Mount Hermon, but elsewhere in the Old Testament it denotes the whole range of the Anti-Lebanon.

ymʾ rbʾ: the Mediterranean.

ḥwrn: the high plateau south of Damascus (cf. Ez. xlvii 16.18), at present the centre of the Druse sect.

gbl: the Edomite mountainous region between the Dead Sea and the Gulf of Aqabah, cf. Psalm lxxxiii 8, usually called Seir in the Old Testament, cf. also line 29.

qdš: probably the Old Testament Kadesh-Barnea.

mdbrʾ rbʾ: the Syrian Desert.

עד קדש וכול מדברא (12) רבא די מדנח חורן ושניר
עד פורת ואמר לי לזרעך אנתן כול ארעא דא
וירתונה לכול עלמים (13) ואשגה זרעך כעפר ארעא
די לא ישכח כול בר אנוש לממניה ואף זרעך לא
יתמנה קום הלך ואזל (14) וחזי כמן ארכהא וכמן
פתיהא ארי לך ולזרעך אנתננה אחריך עד כול עלמיא
(15) ואזלת אנה אברם למסחר ולמחזה ארעא
ושרית למסחר מן גיחון נהרא ואתית ליד ימא עד די
(16) דבקת לטור תורא וסחרת מן ל[יד] ימא רבא
דן די מלחא ואזלת ליד טור תורא למדנחא לפותי
ארעא (17) עד די דבקת לפורת נהרא וסחרת ליד
פורת עד די דבקת לימא שמוקא למדנחא והוית אתה
לי ליד (18) ימא שמוקא עד די דבקת ללשן ים סוף
די נפק מן ימא שמוקא וסחרת לדרומא עד די דבקת

12 *pwrt*: the form of the name is close to the Accadian *Purattu*, while the Old Testament form is *p^{e}rāt*.

13 *yškḥ*: it is interesting to note that the New Testament εὑρίσκειν sometimes has the same connotation, cf. Luke vi 7.

14 *kmn*: cf. XXII, 29; the older form is *kmʾ* or *kmh*, both attested in 1QGenAp.

15 *gyḥwn*: cf. Gen. ii 13, most probably to be identified with the Nile (see note on line 11 and cf. LXX Jer. ii 18; Jub. viii 15; Sirach xxiv 27).

Kadesh and all the Great Desert (12) which is east of Hauran and Senir as far as Euphrates. And He said to me: "To your progeny I will give all this land and they shall inherit it for ever. (13) I will make your progeny as numerous as the dust of the earth which no man finds it possible to number; likewise your progeny shall not be numbered. Come, walk and go, (14) and see what its length and its breadth is, for I will give it to you and to your progeny after you for ever". (15) And I, Abram, set out to travel around and to have a look at the land. I started travelling around from the Gihon River and moved along the Sea until (16) I reached Mount Taurus. Then I travelled from *the shore* of this Great Salt Sea and went along Mount Taurus eastward through the land in its breadth, (17) until I reached the Euphrates River. Then I travelled along the Euphrates until I reached the Red Sea in the east. And I made my way along (18) the Red Sea until I reached the tongue of the Sea of Reeds which flows out from the Red Sea. Then I travelled southward until I reached the

16 *ṭwr twr*ʾ: the Taurus mountain range, called Amanus, in the area of the border between Turkey and Syria. Later rabbinical tradition likewise regarded mount Amanus as the northern border of the promised land, see e.g. Mishnah Shebiith 6, 1.

ymʾ ... *mlḥʾ*: the Mediterranean, cf. line 11.

17 *ymʾ śmwqʾ*: the Indian Ocean. The same designation occurs in Jub. viii 21; ix 2; Eth. Hen. xxxii 2; lxxvii 6-7, and is also used by Herodot and Josephus.

18 *lšn ym swp*: the Red Sea, cf. Jub. viii 14.

גחון (19) נהרא ותבת ואתית לי לביתי בשלם ואשכחת
כול אנשי שלם ואזלת ויתבת באלוני ממרה די בחברון
(20) כלמדנח צפון חברון ובנית תמן מדבח ואסקת
עלוה[י] עלא ומנחא לאל עליון ואכלת ואשתית תמן
(21) אנה וכול אנש ביתי ושלחת קרית לממרה ולערנם
ולאשכול תלתת אחיא אמוראא רחמי ואכלו כחדא
(22) עמי ואשתיו עמי

(23) קדמת יומיא אלן אתה כדרלעומר מלך עילם
אמרפל מלך בבל אריוך מלך כפתוך תדעל מלך
גוים די (24) הוא בין נהרין ועבדו קרב עם ברע מלך
סודם ועם ברשע מלך עומרם ועם שנאב מלך אדמא
(25) ועם שמיאבד מלך צבוין ועם מלך בלע כול אלן
אזדמנו כחדא לקרב לעמקא די סדיא ותקף מלך
(26) עילם ומלכיא די עמה למלך סודם ולכול
חברוהי ושויו עליהון מדא תרתי עשרה שנין הווא

19 *ʾnšy*: singular form with suffix 1st pers. sing.

21 *lmmrh* ... *wlʾškwl*: cf. Gen. xiv 13, where MT reads *ʿānēr* instead of *ʿrnm*, which occurs in the Samaritan Pentateuch as *ʿnrm*.

23 *qdmt*: instead of the common *min qadmat*, the term without *mn* is also attested in Elephantine (COWLEY 30, 17).

kdrlʿwmr etc.: cf. Gen. xiv 1. It is to be noted that here Kedorlaomer is mentioned first, obviously because he is

Gihon (19) River. Then I returned and arrived at my house in safety, and found all my household safe and sound. Thereupon I went to settle at the oaks of Mamre, which is near Hebron, (20) approximately northeast of Hebron. There I built an altar and I offered upon it a burnt offering and a meal offering to God Most High. I ate and drank there, (21) I and all the men of my house, and I sent for Mamre, Arnem and Eshcol, the three Amorite brothers, my friends, and they ate together (22) with me and drank with me.

(23) Before these days Kedorlaomer king of Elam had set out with Amraphel king of Babylon, Arioch king of Cappadocia, and Tidal king of Goyim, which (24) lies between the two rivers, and they had made war against Bera king of Sodom, against Birsha king of Gomorrah, against Shinab king of Admah, (25) against Shemiabad king of Zeboyim and against the king of Bela. All these had joined together for war in the valley of Siddim, and the king of (26) Elam and the kings who were with him had prevailed over the king of Sodom and all his allies, and they had imposed

the leader of the expedition; that Amraphel is called king of Babylon, a contemporary substitute for Shinar; that Arioch is called king of *kptwk* which is most probably to be identified with Cappadocia; and that Goyim, the kingdom of Tidal, is designated as "between the two rivers", i.e. between Tigris and Euphrates.

25 *šmy'bd*: MT reads *šèm'ēbèr*, but the Samaritan Pentateuch has *šm'bd*.

(27) יהבין מדתהון למלך עילם ובשנת תלת עשרה
מרדו בה ובשנת ארבע עשרה דבר מלך עילם לכול
(28) חברוהי וסלקו ארחא די מדברא והווא מחין
ובזין מן פורת נהרא ומחו לרפאיא די בעשתרא (29)
דקרנים ולזומזמיא די בעמן ולאימיא [די ב]שוה
הקריות ולחוריא די בטורי גבל עד דבקו לאיל (30)
פרן די במדברה ותבו ומחו לעין [דינא]
בחצצן תמר (31) ונפק
מלך סודם לעורעהון ומלך [עומרם ומ]לך אדמא
ומלך צבואין ומלך בלע וסדרו(?) קרבא (32) בעמקא
ד[י סדיא] לקובלי כדרל[עומר ומלכיא] די עמה
ואתבר מלך סודום וערק ומלך עומרם (33) נפל
בעגיאין [די] ... ובז

29 *zwmzmy'*: cf. Deut. ii 20. In the translation we follow the usual rendering of Hebrew Biblical names.

30 *wtbw* etc.: this reading of the text seems to be certain on the strength of the remains of letters and on the basis of the fact that the part of the scroll below the gap in line 30 has shrunk. Consequently the remains of letters below the gap are to be combined with those above the gap which appear on the photocopy more to the left. Another consequence of this shrinkage is that the space available between the extant right and left parts of lines 30 ff. is much smaller than suggested by the restoration in the *editio princeps*.

a tribute upon them. Twelve years they had been (27) giving their tribute to the king of Elam, but in the thirteenth year they rebelled against him, and in the fourteenth year the king of Elam led all (28) his allies; they went up by the Way of the Desert and kept smiting and plundering from the Euphrates River onward. They smote the Rephaim who were in Ashteroth (29) Karnaim, the Zamzummim who were in Ammon, the Emim *who were in* Shaveh-Kirjathaim and the Horites who were in the mountains of Gebal, until they reached El- (30) Paran in the Desert. Then they returned and smote the Well of Judgment .... in Hazezon-Tamar.

(31) And the king of Sodom went out to meet them, together with the king of *Gomorrah*, the *k*ing of Admah, the king of Zeboyim and the king of Bela, and prepared for battle (32) in the Valley o*f Siddim* against Kedorla*omer and the kings* who were with him, but the king of Sodom was defeated and he fled, and the king of Gomorrah (33) fell into pits *of* ....

lʿyn dynʾ: a targum rendering of MT *ʿēyn mišpāṭ*, cf. Neofiti 1 ad loc. (Gen. xiv 7).

31 *lʿwrʿhwn*: cf. XXII, 13 and Cowley pp. 269 f. (Behistun 3, 6); *ʿwrʿ* corresponds to *ʿrq* (subst.) in Behistun col. i, 4.10.31, cf. Leander *ÄgAr*, 2 k-o.

32/33 In MT it is said that the kings of both Sodom and Gomorrah fell into the pits (Gen. xiv 10), but, obviously because the king of Sodom figures again in the narrative (XXII, 12), our text only mentions the flight of the king of Sodom and not his falling into a pit, cf. Jub. xiii 22.

מלך עילם כול נכסיא די סודם ודי (34) [עומרם] . . .
. . ש . .]]. . . . . .
. . . . . . ל. . בר אחוי

Col. XXII

(1) די אברם די הוא יתב בסודם כחדא עמהון וכול
נכסוהי ואתה חד מן רעה (2) ענה די יהב אברם ללוט
די פלט מן שביא על אברם ואברם באדין הוא (3) יתב
בחברון וחויה די שבי לוט בר אחוהי וכול נכסוהי
ולא קטיל ודי (4) נגדו מלכיא ארחא חלתא רבתא
למדיתון ושבין ובזין ומחין וקטלין ואזלין (5) למדינת
דרמשק ובכא אברם על לוט בר אחוהי ואתחלם
אברם וקם (6) ובחר מן עבדוהי גברין בחירין לקרב
תלת מאא ותמניאת עשר וערנם (7) ואשכול וממרה
נגדו עמה והוא רדף בתרהון עד דבק לדן ואשכח
אנון (8) שרין בבקעת דן ורמה עליהון בליליא מן
ארבע רוחיהון והווא קטל (9) בהון בליליא ותבר
אנון והוא רדף להון וכולהון הווא ערקין מן קודמוהי

34 *ʾḥwy*: a contracted form of *ʾḥwhy* (see XXII, 3.5.11), cf. Dalman pp. 109 f., 198, and Jastrow s.v. *ʾāb*. The proposed reading *wšbw lwṭ* before *br ʾḥwy* is palaeographically problematic.

..............; and the king of Elam plundered all the riches of Sodom and of (34) *Gomorrah* .... the son of the brother

Col. XXII

(1) of Abram, who dwelt in Sodom, together with them and all his possessions. But one of the shepherds of (2) the flock which Abram had given to Lot, one that had escaped from captivity, came to Abram—Abram at that time dwelt (3) in Hebron—and told him that his nephew Lot was taken captive together with all his possessions, but that he was not killed, and that (4) the kings had taken the Great Valley Road towards their territory, making prisoners, plundering, smiting and killing while making their way (5) to the territory of Damascus. Then Abram wept for his nephew Lot, but Abram braced himself and rose up (6) and chose from among his servants three hundred and eighteen picked soldiers, and Arnem, (7) Eshcol and Mamre went with him. He pursued them until he reached Dan, and he found them (8) encamped in the valley of Dan. He fell upon them by night from all four quarters, perpetrated a slaughter (9) among them during the night, defeated and pursued them, and all of them fled

XXII

1 *ʿmhwn*: the suffix refers to the population of the cities.

4 *ḥltʾ rbtʾ*: the Jordan valley.

mdytwn: < *mdyntwn* < *mdynthwn*.

(10) עד דבקו לחלבון די שימא על שמאל דרמשק
ואצל מנהון כול די שבוא (11) וכול די בזו וכול
טבתהון ואף ללוט בר אחוהי פצא וכול נכסוהי וכול
(12) שביתא די שבאו אתיב ושמע מלך סודם די אתיב
אברם כול שביתא (13) וכול בזתא וסלק לעורעה
ואתה לשלם היא ירושלם ואברם שרא בעמק (14) שוא
והוא עמק מלכא בקעת בית כרמא ומלכיצדק מלכא
דשלם אנפק (15) מאכל ומשתה לאברם ולכול אנשא
די עמה והוא הוא כהן לאל עליון וברך (16) לאברם
ואמר בריך אברם לאל עליון מרה שמיא וארעא
ובריך אל עליון (17) די סגר שנאיך בידך ויהב לה
מעשר מן כול נכסיא די מלך עילם וחברוהי (18)
באדין קרב מלכא די סודם ואמר
לאברם מרי אברם (19) הב לי נפשא די איתי לי די
שביא עמך די אצלתה מן מלך עילם ונכסיא (20)
כולהון שביקין לך אדין אמר

10 *ḥlbwn*: Hobah (Gen. xiv, 15) is here identified with Helbon, a city mentioned in Ez. xxvii 18, some 15 miles north of Damascus, the modern Ḥalbûn.

13 *l'wr'h*: cf. XXI, 31.

šlm: the identification of Salem with Jerusalem already occurs in Ps. lxxvi, 3.

before him (10) until they reached Helbon which is situated north of Damascus. He rescued from them everybody they had taken captive (11) and everything they had taken as booty as well as all their own goods. And he also saved his nephew Lot and all his possessions and (12) all the captives they had taken he brought back. When the king of Sodom learned that Abram had brought back all the captives (13) and all the booty he went up to meet him and came to Salem—that is Jerusalem–, while Abram camped in the valley of (14) Shaveh—that is King's Valley, the plain of Beth-Hakkerem. And Melchizedek, king of Salem, brought out (15) food and drink for Abram and all the men who were with him. He was a priest of God Most High and he blessed (16) Abram and said: "Blessed be Abram by God Most High, Lord of heaven and earth, and blessed be God Most High (17) who has delivered your enemies into your hand". And he gave him a tithe of all the possessions of the king of Elam and his allies. (18)

Thereupon the king of Sodom approached and said to Abram: "My lord Abram, (19) give me the people that are mine who are captives with you, whom you have rescued from the king of Elam, but as far as the possessions, (20) they are all left to

14 *bqʿt byt krmʾ*: probably to be identified with the valley of Ramat Rachel between Jerusalem and Bethlehem.

17 *mn kwl nksyʾ* etc.: the reference to the booty shows that Abram is the subject of the verb *yhb*.

אברם למלך סודם מרים אנה (21) ידי יומא דן לאל
עליון מרה שמיא וארעא אן מן חוט עד ערקא דמסאן
(22) אן אסב מן כול די איתי לך דלמא תהוה אמר
דמן נכסי כול עתרה די (23) אברם ברא מן די
אכלו כבר עולימי די עמי וברא מן חולק תלתת
גבריא די (24) אזלו עמי אנון שליטין בחולקהון למנתן
לך ואתיב אברם כול נכסיא וכול (25) שביתא ויהב
למלך סודם וכול שביא די הואת עמה מן ארעא דא
שבק (26) ושלח כולהון

(27) בתר פתגמיא אלן אתחזי אלהא לאברם בחזוא
ואמר לה הא עשר שנין (28) שלמא מן יום די נפקתה
מן חרן תרתין עבדתה תנה ושבע במצרין וחדא (29)
מן די תבת מן מצרין וכען בקר ומני כול די איתי לך
וחזי כמן כפלין שגיו מן (30) כול די נפקו עמך ביום
מפקך מן חרן וכען אל תדחל אנה עמך ואהוה לך
(31) סעד ותקף ואנה מגן עליך ואספרך לך לתקיף
ברא מנך עתרך ונכסיך (32) ישגון לחדא

25 *mn ʾrʿʾ dʾ*: apparently the region of the Dead Sea. In contradistinction to the captives of Sodom, mentioned at the beginning of the line, here all the remaining captives are meant.

you". Then Abram said to the king of Sodom: "I lift up (21) my hand this day unto God Most High, Lord of heaven and earth, that from thread to sandalstrip (22) I will not take anything from all what is yours—lest you should say: 'From my possession comes all of (23) Abram's wealth'—except for what my men, who are with me, have already eaten, and except for the portion of the three men who (24) went with me: they themselves are the disposers of their portion to offer you a gift". So Abram restored all the possessions and all (25) the captives and gave them to the king of Sodom; he also set free all the captives from this region who were with him (26) and let them all go.

(27) After these events God appeared to Abram in a vision and said to him: "Look, ten years (28) have passed since you departed from Haran: two you have spent here, seven in Egypt and one (29) since you returned from Egypt. Well now, examine and count all that is yours, and see how it has grown to be double (30) of all which came out with you when you departed from Haran. And now, do not fear: I am with you and I am to you (31) both support and strength, and I am a shield over you and a screen to you against him that is stronger than you; your wealth and your possessions (32)

27 *ʾtḥzy*: the scribe first wrote *ʾtḥzyw* but afterwards corrected this scribal error by putting a dot above and below the *waw*.

31 *ʾsprk*: a Persian loanword, cf. W. W. Müller, *RQum* II, 1959-1960, pp. 445-447.

ואמר אברם מרי אלהא שגי לי עתר ונכסין ולמא לי
(33) כול אלן ואנה כדי אמות ערטלי אהך די לא
בנין וחד מן בני ביתי ירתנני (34) אליעזר בר[
]לד .רתני ואמר לה לא ירתנך דן להן די יפוק

shall increase exceedingly". But Abram said: "My Lord God, numerous indeed are my wealth and possessions, but of what avail are (33) all these things to me, seeing that, when I die, I shall go hence barren, without children, and one of those born in my house shall inherit me, (34) Eliezer the son of ....!" But He said to him: "This one shall not inherit you, but he that shall come forth

THE PRAYER OF NABONIDUS FROM CAVE 4
(4QOrNab)

INTRODUCTION

In 1955 four fragments of a hitherto unknown text belonging to the Daniel-cycle were discovered in cave 4 of Qumran. On the strength of the first words of the text the first editor, J. T. MILIK, called it 'The Prayer of Nabonidus' (4QOr(atio)Nab). Three fragments together form parts of the beginning of the writing; the fourth fragment contains a number of words from a subsequent section, probably from a following column.

Judged by the script, these fragments come from a document written at the beginning of the Christian era, but the writing itself might be some centuries older. The language of 4QOrNab corresponds significantly with that of Daniel, and the contents of the fragments remind us immediately of Daniel 4. On the basis of the fragmentary text MEYER has defended the thesis that this writing represents a phase of literary tradition preceding that of the story in its present form as related in Daniel 4. In his opinion the earliest tradition, as evidenced by 4QOrNab, only knew the dream about the world tree and its interpretation. This thesis is based on a reconstruction of the text with which we disagree on many points in our edition. If one reads in line 3 "and so I became like the animals", there is no reason to suppose that the 4QOrNab tradition differs significantly from that of Daniel 4, the more so if *hḥwy* in line 5 is taken as an imperative and not as an indicative. This means that 4QOrNab line 6 ff. is a royal proclamation, like Daniel iii 31 ff.

It is fairly safe to assume that the original Nabonidus tradition (king of Babylon, 555-539) was transferred in Daniel to the well-known Nebuchadnezzar II, king of Babylon (604-562), and that the 'seer, a Jewish man' was not yet identified with Daniel in 4QOrNab. This shows that the present text represents an earlier stage in the tradition history of Daniel iii 31-iv 34 (cf. also the reference to Teman, line 2). Judged by the contents, there is no essential difference between the 4QOrNab tradition and that of the book of Daniel, at least so far as these fragments allow us to draw any conclusions.

LITERATURE

Text Publication:

J. T. MILIK, "Prière de Nabonide" et autres écrits d'un cycle de Daniel. Fragments araméens de Qumrân 4, *RB* 63 (1956), pp. 407-415.

Further Literature:

J. D. AMUSIN, The Qumran Fragment of the "Prayer" of King Nabonidus of Babylonia, *Vestnik Drevnej Istorii* 1958 no. 4 (no. 66), pp. 104-117. [Russian].

J. D. AMUSIN, *The Texts of Qumran I*, Moscow 1971, pp. 326-335. [Russian]

D. S. ATTEMA, Het gebed van Nabonidus, in: *Schrift en Uitleg*. Studies ... aangeboden aan Prof. Dr. W. H. Gispen, Kampen 1970, pp. 7-20.

J. CARMIGNAC- É. COTHENET- H. LIGNÉE, *Les textes de Qumrân traduits et annotés* II, Paris 1963, pp. 289-294 (by J. CARMIGNAC).

W. DOMMERSHAUSEN, *Nabonid im Buche Daniel*, Mainz 1964.

A. Dupont-Sommer, *Les écrits esséniens découverts près de la mer Morte*, Paris 1959, pp. 291-306.

D. N. Freedman, The Prayer of Nabonidus, *BASOR* 145 (1957), pp. 31-32.

C. M. I. Gevaryahu, The Qumran Fragments of the Prayer of Nabonid, in: J. Liver (ed.), *Iyyunim limgillot midbar y^ehudah*. Lectures Delivered at the 3rd Annual Conference (1957) in Memory of E. L. Sukenik, Jerusalem 1957, pp. 12-23. [Hebrew]

A. Mertens, *Das Buch Daniel im Lichte der Texte vom Toten Meer* (Stuttgarter Biblische Monographien 12), Echter Verlag/Katholisches Bibelwerk, Würzburg/Stuttgart 1971, pp. 34-42.

R. Meyer, *Das Gebet des Nabonid*. Eine in den Qumran-Handschriften wiederentdeckte Weisheitserzählung, Akademie-Verlag, Berlin 1962 (= Sitzungsberichte der sächsischen Akademie der Wissenschaften zu Leipzig, Phil.-hist. Kl. 107/3).

E. Vogt, Precatio regis Nabonid in pia narratione judaica (4Q), *Bibl* 37 (1956), pp. 532-534.

I

(1) מלי צ[ל]תא די צלי נבני מלך א[רעא די בב]ל
מלכא] רבא כדי כתיש הוא] (2) בשחנא באישא
בפתגמ א]להא עלי]א בתימן[מדינתא בשחנא
באישא] (3) כתיש הוית שנין שבע וכן[לחיותא] שוי

I

1 The name *nbny* is the Accadian personal name Nabû-nā'id, shortened on the analogy of Hebrew-Aramaic hypocoristic names such as Mattay, Zakkay etc., cf. DALMAN, pp. 178 f.
Instead of the reading *mlk 'twr wbbl* « king of Assyria and Babylon » (proposed by MILIK, MEYER, AMUSIN, MERTENS *et al.*), a phrase occurring neither in the Old Testament nor in related literature, we prefer to read with DUPONT-SOMMER and CARMIGNAC « king of the land of Babylon », in view of the expressions *mlk' dy bbl* Ezra v 13; *mlk bbl* Dan. vii 1; Ezra v 12, cf. Dan. i 1; Ezra ii 1; Is. xiv 4, and *'r'' dbbl* TJ Jer. l 28.
mlk' rb': cf. Dan. ii 10; Sefire I B, 7, and Accadian *šarru rabû* "the great king".
ktyš hw': for this conjecture (with a finite verb instead of the participle, read by MILIK *et al.*) cf. line 3 and 6. For the use of *ktš* in a similar sense, cf. 1QGenAp XX, 16 f.; 11QtgJob XXIX, 3.

2 *šḥn'*: cf. 11QtgJob XVI, 2.
'lh' 'ly': cf. Dan. iii 26.32 etc. Other possible readings are *'lh šmy'* « God of heaven », cf. Dan. ii 19.37, and *'lh 'lhy'* « God of gods », cf. Dan. ii 47.
tymn mdynt': for this type of construction cf. Ezra v 8; vi 2. Teman (LXX Θαιμάν) is the Biblical *Tēymā'*, Acc. *Tema*, Arab. *Taima*, a North-Arabian desert city. For Nabonidus' stay in Tema see *ANET*, pp. 306.312 ff.,

I

(1) The words of the p*ra*yer said by Nabonidus the king of *the* la*nd Bab*ylon, the *great* king, *when he was smitten* (2) with malignant boils by the ordinance of G*od Most Hig*h in *the city of* Teman: *With malignant boils* (3) I was smitten for seven years, and so I came to be li*ke the animals*; *but I prayed to God Most*

ANET Suppl. pp. 126 f., and cf. *HUCA* 19, 1945-1946, pp. 405-489 (J. Lewy); *AJA* 59, 1955, pp. 315-318 (B. Segall).

3 « Seven years »: cf. Dan. iv 13.20.22.29.
wkn [lḥywtʾ] šwy ʾ[nh]: the reading and interpretation of this passage are problematic. Several authors read *wmn* instead of *wkn*, conjecturing in the lacuna *ʾnšyʾ* (Milik, Mertens *et al.*) « far away from men », or *krsyy* (Meyer, Attema) « far from my throne », taking *šwy* to be the (elsewhere unattested) participle peal of *šwʾ* II which means in the pael « to place ». Gevaryahu proposes to read *wbqrʾ hwyt šwy ʾnh* « and I came to be like the beasts ». For palaeographical reasons, however, the reading *wkn* « and so » appears to be preferable to *wmn* « and from », whereas the conjecture *wbqrʾ* must be excluded, since, in view of the space available, the third letter cannot possibly be a *q*. Taking *šwy* to be the peîl of *šwʾ* I (cf. Dan. v 21 $k^{e}tib$) « to be like » we conjecture *lḥywtʾ* on the strength of Dan. v 21.
ṣlyt qdm ʾlhʾ ʿlyʾ: this conjecture is based on the fact that the subject of *šbq* in line 4, which must certainly be God, makes it inevitable that there was some reference to Him in the lost words at the end of line 3. In addition to this it is most probable that the reference to God's forgiveness presupposes some reference to a human act recognizing His supremacy.

א]נה וצלית קדם אלהא עליא] (4) וחטאי שבק לה
גזר והוא] גבר]יהודי מ[ן בני גלותא והוא אמר לי[
(5) החוי וכתב למעבד יקר ור[בו והדר] לשם א[להא
עליא וכן כתבת כדי] (6) כתיש הוית בשחנא ב[אישא
בתימן[בפתגם אלהא עליא] (7) שנין
שבע מצלא הוי[ת ושבחת ל]אלהי כספא ודהבא
[נחשא פרזלא] (8) אעא אבנא חספא מן די[

4 *wḥṭ'y šbq*: the verb *šbq* used in connection with a word for sin commonly expresses the idea of forgiving, e.g. 11QtgJob XXXVIII, 2, which means that « He pardoned my sins » is the most natural translation here. Accordingly *lh* must not be connected with the preceding words, in which case one has either to suppose a *dativus ethicus* (which is most unlikely here), or a pronominal object referring to *wḥṭ'y* "and my sin" (which would rather presuppose *wlḥṭ'y*), or a *dativus commodi* (which makes a change of the text from *lh* to *ly* inevitable, cf. MILIK).

lh gzr: a nominal sentence in which the suffix in *lh* must refer to the subject of *šbq*, which is God.

The noun *gzr*, literally « divider », occurs in Dan. ii 27; iv 4; v 7.11 and means « diviner ».

gbr . . . *glwt'*: cf. Dan. ii 25; v 13.

whw' 'mr ly: for this conjecture see the following note.

5 The verbal forms *hḥwy* and *ktb* as such can be explained either as perfects or as imperatives. Since the text as a whole appears to be a royal proclamation similar to that of Nebuchadnezzar in Dan. iii 31-iv 34 (this is confirmed by the use of the haphel of *ḥw'* in the present text, cf. Dan. iii 32), the promulgation of the edict can only be ascribed to the king. Therefore the subject of the verbal forms, understood as perfects, cannot possibly be the

High (4) and He pardoned my sins. He had a diviner, who was a Jewish *man* fr*om the exiles, and who said to me*: (5) Make a written proclamation that honour, gr*eatness and glory* be given to the name of G*od Most High. And so I wrote*: *When* (6) I was smitten with ma*lignant* boils .... in Teman *by the ordinance of God Most High* (7) for seven years, *I* prayed *and gave praise to* the gods of silver and gold, *bronze, iron,* (8) wood, stone and clay, since .... that th*ey* were gods ....

diviner; it cannot be the king either, for this would require the first person singular. The only possibility is to consider the verbal forms to be imperatives. It also follows that it is the diviner who commands the king to proclaim and to write. In view of this the end of line 4 must have contained a phrase introducing this command.
yqr wrbw whdr: cf. Dan. v 18.
The end of the line must have contained a phrase introducing Nabonidus' written proclamation. Therefore we propose to read *wkn ktbt.*

6 *hwyt*: 1st pers. sing., referring to the king, on the basis of our argumentation in the note on line 5.
bptgm ʾlhʾ ʿlyʾ: reconstruction on the strength of line 2, a phrase which is too long to fit in the preceding lacuna, since in the manuscript *btymn* appears directly below *lšm* in line 5.

7/8 *wšbḥt*: the first lacuna in line 7 has been filled out with this verb because it also appears in Dan. v 4.23 in connection with « gods of silver, gold, etc. »; the author added *ḥspʾ* to the sequence of materials, cf. Dan. ii 33.45.
The lacuna after *mn dy* seems to have contained at least one letter more than *hwyt sbr* proposed by Meyer, Dupont-Sommer, Carmignac (or *hwyt ʾmr*), therefore we suggest to read *hwyt msbr*, taking *msbr* to be an aphel or pael participle.

]ר די אלהין ה[מון [(9a)]או.[
]דר[ ]..ל.[ ].[
(9)]מי ...[

II

(1) מ]לבר המון
(2) [אחלמת [ ]..נה אח[ ].[ ].לם
]של (3)].[ ]נו
רחמי לא יכלת[[(4) כמה
דמא אנתה ל.[

9a This line has been added afterwards as a scribal correction between lines 8 and 9.

II

1-4 In view of the handwriting this fragment belongs to the

... (9a) ....
....
.... (9) ....
....

II

1 .... *ap*art from these I dreamt 2 ....
....

3 .... my intestines. I could not ....
....

4 How much are you like ... .

same document but may come from another column. The poor state of the text makes it impossible to reconstruct its contents and to interpret its meaning.